Staying Safe Online

PEARSON

Harlow, England • London • New York • Boston • San Francisco • Toronto • Sydney • Auckland • Singapore • Hong Kong
Tokyo • Seoul • Taipei • New Delhi • Cape Town • São Paulo • Mexico City • Madrid • Amsterdam • Munich • Paris • Milan

PEARSON EDUCATION LIMITED

Edinburgh Gate
Harlow CM20 2JE
Tel: +44 (0)1279 623623
Fax: +44 (0)1279 431059
Website: www.pearson.com/uk

First published in Great Britain in 2012

Pearson Education is not responsible for the content of third-party internet sites.

ISBN: 978-0-273-77473-0

British Library Cataloguing-in-Publication Data
A catalogue record for this book is available from the British Library

Library of Congress Cataloging-in-Publication Data
Ballew, Joli.
   Staying safe online in simple steps / Joli Ballew.
      p. cm.
   ISBN 978-0-273-77473-0 (pbk.)
   1. Computer networks--Security measures--Popular works. 2. World Wide Web--Security measures--Popular works. 3. Internet--Safety measures--Popular works. I. Title.
   TK5105.59.B355 2012
   005.8--dc23
                              2012016015

10 9 8 7 6 5 4 3 2 1
16 15 14 13 12

Typeset in 11/14pt ITC Stone Sans by 3
Printed and bound in Great Britain by Scotprint, Haddington, East Lothian

Staying Safe Online

in Simple steps

Joli Ballew

Dedication and acknowledgements

For my wonderful friends, colleagues, readers and family; be safe out there!

Author's acknowledgements

I want to thank Steve Temblett and Robert Cottee for once again choosing me to write another In Simple Steps book. I've lost count, but I think we're nearing a dozen or so. I really like writing these books, and I especially enjoy writing for my contemporaries, my over-fifties audience. I thank you for purchasing this book and placing your trust in me to teach you how to stay safe online. I'd also like to thank my copy editors, technical editors, layout technicians, and others involved in the book writing process. These include Laura Blake, Linda Dhondy and Geoff Chatterton. All of these people make sure that the text is accurate, that the grammar is correct, and that the images are placed properly in the text, among other things. I could not do it without them.

I would also like to thank my agent, Neil Salkind, Ph.D., from the Salkind Literary Agency. We've been together for a decade, and during that time we've managed to publish 40+ books together. Over the years, we've become friends too. And finally, I'd like to acknowledge my family, including my dad, my daughter Jennifer, her husband Andrew, and my partner Cosmo. They are very supportive of me and of my work and I appreciate and love them dearly.

Publisher's acknowledgements

We are grateful to the following for permission to reproduce copyright material:

Figures
Figure on page 191 from Cybercrime top 20 countries. Google images. http://www.enigmasoftware.com/top-20-countries-the-most-cybercrime.

Screenshots
Screenshot on page 170 from AOL/AIM; Screenshots on pages 151 and 152 from Blogger.Ed; Screenshots on pages 40, 68, 82, 127, 134, 158, 170, 200 from Facebook; Screenshots on pages 40, 68, 82, 127, 134, 140, 158, 170, 200 from Facebook; Screenshots on pages 22, 56, 81, 82, 83, 101, 103, 128, 133, 155, 156, 159, 163, 164, 191 from Google; Screenshots on pages 165, 166 and 167 from Lavasoft; Screenshot on page 114 from Trusted Shops; Screenshots on pages 19 and 119 from Visa Inc.; Screenshots on page 153 from YouTube; Screenshots on pages 73, 84, 89, 102 reproduced with permission of Yahoo! © 2012 Yahoo! Inc. YAHOO! and the YAHOO! logo are registered trademarks of Yahoo! Inc.

Microsoft screen shots reprinted with permission from Microsoft Corporation.

In some instances we have been unable to trace the owners of copyright material, and we would appreciate any information that would enable us to do so.

Contents at a glance

Use online products and services with confidence

Get to grips with using online products and services confidently with minimal time, fuss and bother.

In Simple Steps guides guarantee immediate results. They tell you everything you need to know on a specific application; from the most essential tasks to master, to every activity you'll want to accomplish, through to solving the most common problems you'll encounter.

Helpful features

To build your confidence and help you to get the most out of the internet, practical hints, tips and shortcuts feature on every page:

ALERT: Explains and provides practical solutions to the most commonly encountered problems

HOT TIP: Time and effort saving shortcuts

SEE ALSO: Points you to other related tasks and information

DID YOU KNOW? Additional features to explore

WHAT DOES THIS MEAN?
Jargon and technical terms explained in plain English

Practical. Simple. Fast.

in Simple steps

Contents

Top 10 Staying Safe Online Tips

1 Introduction to internet safety

4 Avoiding spam

5 Using alternative web browsers

8 Using social networking sites safely

9 Sharing your personal information on the web

10 Exploring free software

11 Keeping children and grandchildren safe

12 Dealing with cyberbullying, cybercrime and cyberstalking

13 Securing your computer and network

Top 10 Staying Safe Online Problems Solved

Top 10 Staying Safe Online Tips

Tip 1: Create strong passwords for websites

You must create user names and passwords for many of the websites you visit, including social networking sites, banking institutions, shopping websites and others. Those passwords should be hard to guess, and they should be different for each site you log in to.

- Create passwords that are at least six characters long.
- Include upper and lower case letters.
- Include at least one number.
- Include one or more special symbols.
- Create passwords that you can remember with a little effort, like MyAccountAtAmaz0n74.
- Don't opt to let websites keep you logged in.

ALERT: If someone learns the password you set for, say, a savings and loan account, they'll try that same password at other places too, like investing websites, shopping websites and others. That's why it's important to use different passwords for every website (and different user names, if possible).

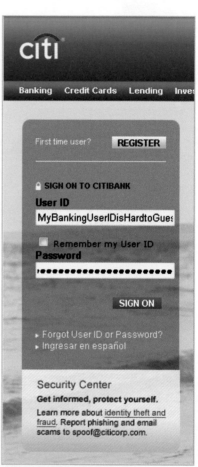

? DID YOU KNOW?
No matter how well you protect your own passwords or how difficult they are to guess, your user name and password can still be stolen if there's a security breach at the institution (e.g. a bank) that stores them.

🔥 HOT TIP: People whose business it is to steal passwords will try passwords like this first: password, 12345, abcde, and letmein. They may also try your birthday, children's names and pet's names too.

Tip 3: Know common signs of scam emails

There are some things that are common to emails from people that are out to scam you. Misspelled words are a dead giveaway, as is bad grammar and poorly written text. You can rest assured that email from your bank won't have any typographical errors in it. Here are some additional signs:

- Someone wants you to send them money.
- You are asked to provide (for whatever reason), personally identifiable information such as a National Insurance number, user name or password.
- The email originated in Nigeria or other foreign country and/or there are a lot of capital letters in the email.

Subject **FROM UNITED STATES AMBASSADOR TO NIGERIA**

To Joli Ballew ☆

To: undisclosed-recipients:
Subject: FROM UNITED STATES AMBASSADOR TO NIGERIA

UNITED STATES AMBASSADOR TO NIGERIA
U.S. DEPARTMENT OF STATE
BUREAU OF CONSULAR AFFAIRS
U.S AMBASSADOR TO NIGERIA
11 GARIK ROAD ABUJA

Attention beneficiary,

My name is Terence Patrick McCulley, the new United States amba
senate had confirmed my nomination on august 5th 2010 after being

- The sender claims to be royalty, a distant relative, a prison inmate looking for friendship, or a young woman looking for love.
- Your email program sends the email to the Junk or Spam folder, or denotes the email with a distinct warning.

! ALERT: Never respond to emails you believe to be scams, even out of curiosity or to inconvenience the sender.

● The sender's email address is invalid or complex.

From ELİTAŞKLAR.COM <c34kTmNtz7YtAuxTY0MIL5@konuk.net>
Subject **nurgul - sarsilarak bosalmak istiyorum**
To joli_ballew@hotmail.com☆

 Junk Mail

-
Sayin uyemiz, Bir yeni mesaj aldiniz!
Alt kisimlarda bulunmakta olan bilgilerle siteye hesabiniza erisebilirsiniz.

Email : joli_ballew@hotmail.com
Sifre : 123456789

Otomatik Giriş için Tıklayın!

ELİTAŞKLAR.COM

● Your email program suggests the email is a scam.

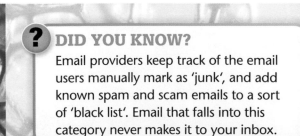

This message may be a scam.
Disable scam detection for all messages   Ignore Warning

? DID YOU KNOW?
Email providers keep track of the email users manually mark as 'junk', and add known spam and scam emails to a sort of 'black list'. Email that falls into this category never makes it to your inbox.

Tip 4: Explore your web browser's safety and security options

All web browsers offer safety and security options. What's available and how to configure the options differ from browser to browser, but all have similar characteristics and purposes.

1 The security options generally offer a way to define the level of security you need. The default setting is generally appropriate.

2 Privacy options often offer a way to stop websites from tracking your movements on the web.

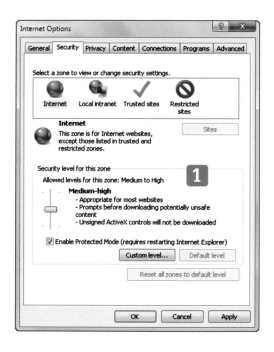

3 Other options include the ability to stop pop-up advertisements, warn you of potentially harmful websites, start a private browsing session where no cookies or history are tracked, and more.

4 Some browsers even offer parental controls (or grand-parental controls!).

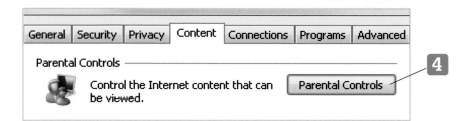

Tip 5: Don't click ads!

Advertisements can be dangerous. Clicking a pop-up advertisement could invoke a worm or virus. Clicking an advertisement on a web page could take you to a site that is unsafe, is a phishing website, or one that is laden with viruses, adware, malware and other threats. You'll find advertisements in various places, and it's important to avoid all of them.

1 When you search for something from a website such as Google, Yahoo!, Bing and others, often the first few search results listed are paid ads. Scroll down until you get to the real results.

2 Ads appear on the right side of search results too, as well as on web pages you personalise.

3 Ads can appear in pop-up windows. Never click these ads, only click the X to close them.

4 Ads appear on social networking sites often in the right-hand column.

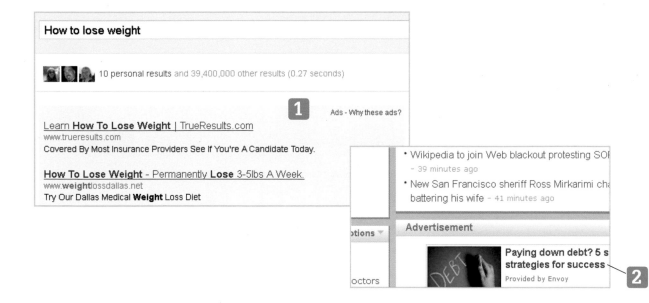

 ALERT: Do not click ads in email you receive.

 SEE ALSO: Enable a Pop-Up Blocker, in Chapter 6.

ALERT: If you accidentally click a pop-up advertisement and then other pop-ups begin to appear, you probably have just unleashed a virus!

Tip 6: Learn what you should never share online

One of the first things to know about staying safe when using social websites is what not to share with others. Here are a few things you should never share anywhere, including Facebook, Twitter, LinkedIn and similar websites.

- Your physical address or phone number.
- Credit card, banking or financial information.
- When you'll be away on holiday and for how long (if you must post, always state you have a house sitter).
- When you're leaving your home unattended.
- The full names, ages, addresses and so on, of your children, friends or relatives.
- Pictures of new, expensive purchases.
- How much you dislike your boss or coworkers.

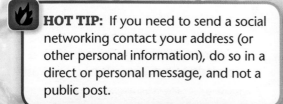
HOT TIP: If you need to send a social networking contact your address (or other personal information), do so in a direct or personal message, and not a public post.

? DID YOU KNOW?
Although it's unlikely a friend or acquaintance would rob your home while you're on holiday, their unruly children might!

Tip 9: Log off or lock your computer

When you sit down at your computer you probably open your email program, log in to Facebook or LinkedIn, open folders that contain your personal files and so on. If you walk away from your computer without logging off or locking it, anyone can sit down in front of it and access both your online data and personal data stored on your computer. You should always log off or lock the computer when you're going to move away from it.

1 On a Windows-based computer, click the Start button.

2 Click the right-arrow shown here.

3 Click Lock or Log off.

HOT TIP: Hopefully you'll follow the advice in this book and create password-protected user accounts for everyone you want to have access to your computer. Refer to Chapter 11 to learn how.

? DID YOU KNOW?
It's faster to get back to work if you choose Lock vs. Log off.

WHAT DOES THIS MEAN?

Log off: when you *log off* your computer, you make it available for someone else to log on to it.

Lock: when you *lock* the computer you leave programs and files open, but enable the lock screen. Either way, if your account is password-protected, you must type the password to gain access again.

Tip 10: Check for and resolve security issues

Windows 7 computers offer a unique way to check for and resolve security issues through the Action Center. Most problems identified in the Action Center also come with a suggestion to fix the problem.

1 Click Start, and click Control Panel.

2 In Category view, shown here, click Review your computer's status.

Adjust your computer's settings   View by: Category ▼

System and Security
Review your computer's status
Back up your computer
Find and fix problems

Network and Internet
View network status and tasks

User Accounts and Family Safety
Add or remove user accounts
Set up parental controls for any user

Appearance and Personalization
Change the theme
Change desktop background

3 Review any issues shown in red or yellow as well as their solutions.

4 Apply solutions as applicable.

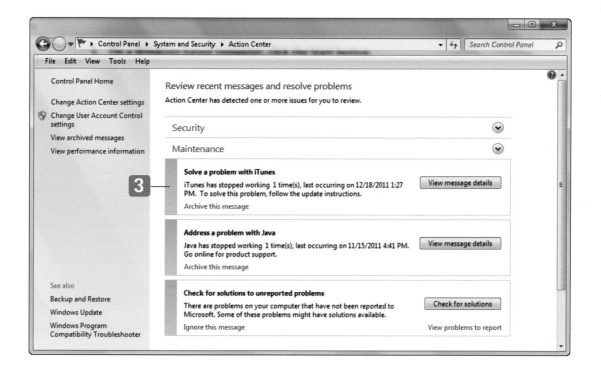

HOT TIP: Check the Action Center once a month to make sure your computer is in tip-top condition.

ALERT: If you see a pop-up appear on your screen and you aren't sure if it originated from the Action Center, don't click it! Instead, open the Action Center to see if anything needs attention.

Create strong passwords for websites

You must create user names and passwords for many of the websites you visit, including social networking sites, banking institutions, shopping websites and others. Those passwords should be hard to guess, and they should be different for each site you log in to.

- Create passwords that are at least six characters long.
- Include upper and lower case letters.
- Include at least one number.
- Include one or more special symbols.
- Create passwords that you can remember with a little effort, like MyAccountAtAmaz0n74.
- Don't opt to let websites keep you logged in.

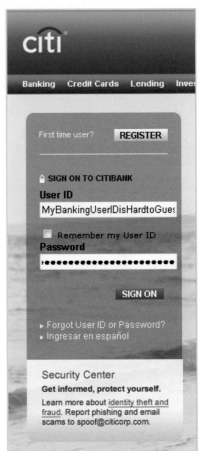

 ALERT: If someone learns the password you set for, say, a savings and loan account, they'll try that same password at other places too, like investing websites, shopping websites and others. That's why it's important to use different passwords for every website (and different user names, if possible).

DID YOU KNOW?
No matter how well you protect your own passwords or how difficult they are to guess, your user name and password can still be stolen if there's a security breach at the institution (e.g. a bank) that stores them.

HOT TIP: People whose business it is to steal passwords will try passwords like this first: password, 12345, abcde, and letmein. They may also try your birthday, children's names and pet's names too.

Protect your list of passwords

You'll have to keep your passwords written down in a list. You'll also have to keep that list safe. Consider the damage a person could do with a list of user names and passwords! Here are some tips for protecting that list.

- Keep user names in one list and passwords in another, and keep the two lists in separate places.
- Put the list in a folder that is amid others, and name the folder something like Pet Health Records or My Favourite Recipes.
- When writing down your passwords, don't write down the entire password. For instance, if your password is MyDogHasFleez#, only write down MyDogHasFleez. This will work provided you always add a # to the end of every password!
- Consider storing passwords in a secure folder on the internet, like in Google Documents, shown here. Then, should you need to access that list you only need to remember one password, the one that takes you to this folder.

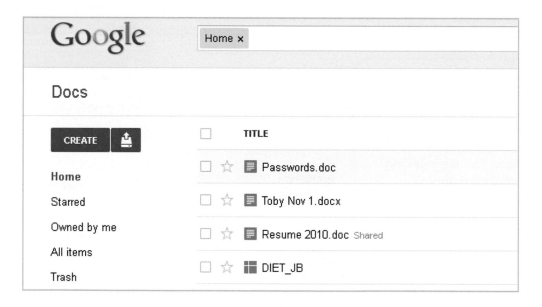

! ALERT: If your house is ever robbed or your computer ever stolen, change all of your internet user names and passwords. Thieves don't just want your physical valuables anymore; they want your virtual valuables too.

 HOT TIP: If you've never tried Google Documents, visit www.google.com, and under More, click Documents to get started.

Install anti-virus software

You must protect your computer from viruses. You can acquire viruses from email, from websites or even from office documents that contain macros (computer code that automates tasks). There's no way to avoid viruses forever, no matter how careful you are. You *must* install anti-virus software.

1 Purchase or download anti-virus software. Consider Microsoft Security Essentials, shown here.

2 Follow the instructions to install that software.

3 When prompted, configure the software to get updates regularly, if possible, each night.

HOT TIP: Microsoft Security Essentials is free and is quite effective against viruses and other internet threats.

ALERT: Never install anti-virus software from a company you've never heard of! Likewise, never run free virus scans. Most of these 'companies' will place viruses (real or fake) on your computer and urge you to purchase their software to rid the computer of them.

4 Configure the software to run scans regularly too.

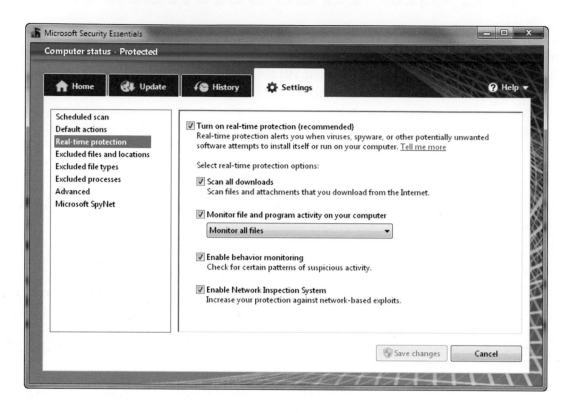

WHAT DOES THIS MEAN?

Virus: a virus is harmful computer code that can cause your computer to act erratically, send out email as you, post to social networks as you, and spread to other computers without your knowledge.

Avoid common email scams

You're going to get email from people you do not know; this is called junk mail or spam. A lot of this email will resemble the junk mail that you get in the post. It will claim you've won a prize, are the recipient of an inheritance, or ask you to reply with personal information, such as your bank account numbers. Some email providers offer a spam or junk folder, shown here, where email they think is junk mail gets sent automatically.

- Banks and financial institutions, the government and investment companies never ask you to send personal information or account numbers via email.
- Your mortgage company will not ask you to send or verify account numbers, ask for your date of birth or want you to verify your password.
- No trusted entity will ask you to reply with your user name and/or password for verification purposes.
- If you inherit some money or win the lottery, you'll get a certified letter, not an email.
- No person from Nigeria knows you and wants to give you money.
- If an email has a typographical error in it, and it's supposed to be from a professional institution, it's a fraud.

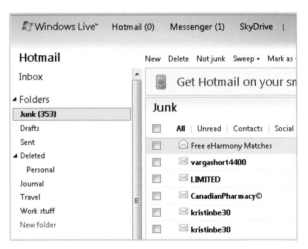

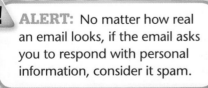

ALERT: Never click a link in any email you even slightly suspect to be spam.

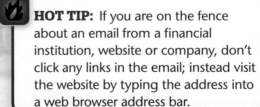

ALERT: No matter how real an email looks, if the email asks you to respond with personal information, consider it spam.

HOT TIP: If you are on the fence about an email from a financial institution, website or company, don't click any links in the email; instead visit the website by typing the address into a web browser address bar.

Don't open email attachments (yet)

Some email arrives with more than text. It may include a picture, a short video or a document, for instance. That extra information is 'attached'. You should only open attachments from people you know, and even then you should be sceptical. Viruses are most often spread through emails, and you may have received the attachment from a friend's computer that is infected.

1 Note that an email has an attachment. You'll see a paperclip icon.

2 Locate the attachment in the email. Here's it's a document that is a PDF, a common file type for official correspondence.

3 Often you can click or double-click the attachment to view or to open it; for now, refrain from doing so.

4 Most of the time you can right-click an attachment to save it or perform other tasks.

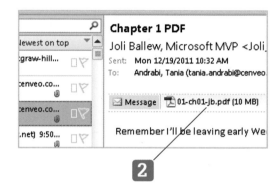

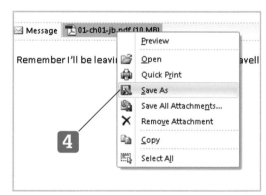

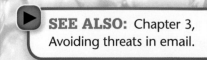

SEE ALSO: Chapter 3, Avoiding threats in email.

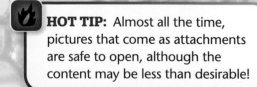

HOT TIP: Almost all the time, pictures that come as attachments are safe to open, although the content may be less than desirable!

Know how to perform web searches

There are a lot of places you can search for information on the web. You can search from www.google.com, www.bing.com, www.yahoo.com and more. In fact, you can search from the Address bar in most web browsers. It is best to search with established search providers, though. Once you're ready to search, keep the following things in mind to obtain effective results.

1 Avoid using words in your search that can be, in another context, sexual.

2 Don't click the results listed first; those are ads. Scroll down a bit to the actual results.

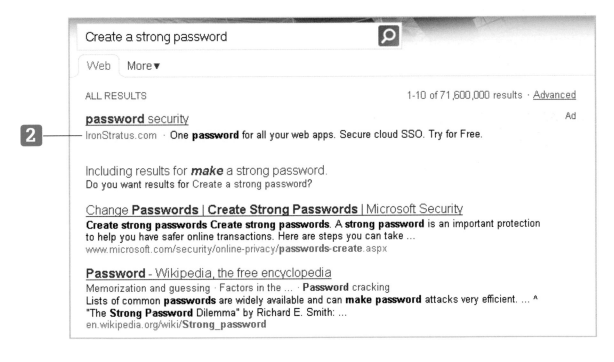

2

Create a strong password   🔍

Web   More ▼

ALL RESULTS   1-10 of 71,600,000 results · Advanced

password security   Ad
IronStratus.com · One **password** for all your web apps. Secure cloud SSO. Try for Free.

Including results for **make** a strong password.
Do you want results for Create a strong password?

Change **Passwords** | **Create Strong Passwords** | Microsoft Security
Create strong passwords Create strong passwords. A **strong password** is an important protection to help you have safer online transactions. Here are steps you can take ...
www.microsoft.com/security/online-privacy/**passwords-create**.aspx

Password - Wikipedia, the free encyclopedia
Memorization and guessing · Factors in the ... · **Password** cracking
Lists of common **passwords** are widely available and can **make password** attacks very efficient. ... ^
"The **Strong Password** Dilemma" by Richard E. Smith: ...
en.wikipedia.org/wiki/**Strong_password**

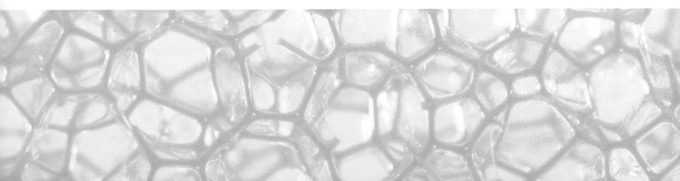

3 Note the source of the information in the result you like, and make sure it's from a trusted source.

4 Before clicking, try to get a preview of the information. Some search engines, like Bing, offer a right-facing arrow that will show you a preview of the page and you won't have to click it.

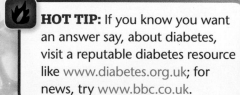

ALERT: Common and trusted results pages can be from Microsoft, CNN, Apple, Wikipedia, Amazon, Google, Yahoo, WebMD and similar well-known entities, although results you'll find in user-submitted 'answers' and 'forums' can't always be trusted.

HOT TIP: If you know you want an answer say, about diabetes, visit a reputable diabetes resource like www.diabetes.org.uk; for news, try www.bbc.co.uk.

Avoid phishing emails

Spammers often create official looking correspondence from financial institutions and shopping websites to lure you to a fake website, often one that looks much like the official one, to try to trick you into entering your personal information. Once you do, the spammers steal that information. This is called phishing. There's one sure way to avoid this, verify that the link in an official looking email really takes you to the website it's supposed to.

1 Open any email that contains a link to a web page.

2 Hover your mouse over the link.

3 If the link matches the site you want to visit, you can safely click it. If it does not, as shown here, you know it's a 'phishing' email.

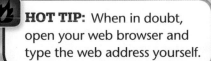

http://www.iwillstealyouridentity.com/
Click to follow link

www.amazon.com

HOT TIP: When in doubt, open your web browser and type the web address yourself.

ALERT: It's really best never to click a link like this in an email. It only takes a second or two to open a web browser and type in an address, or choose it from a list of favourites or bookmarks.

Look for the 's' before making an online purchase

Before you make purchases from any website, make sure that the site can be trusted with your credit card information and other personal data. You can check easily by looking for https:// in the Address bar. If you don't see the 's', don't enter any personal data.

1 When you're ready to make a purchase, note what is listed in the Address bar of your web browser window.

2 If you see https://, shown here, it's okay to make the purchase.

3 If you only see http://, do *not* enter any personal information.

HOT TIP: Many websites now let you pay with PayPal, a secure way to perform online transactions. Setting up a PayPal account takes a little time, but you only have to do it once!

! ALERT: Before you make purchases from a person on eBay or a similar website, make sure that person has good reviews and has been doing business at the site for a good amount of time.

? DID YOU KNOW?
The s after https means the website has taken steps to get a 'certificate' from a certificate authority, and that authority has deemed the site safe for handling your personal information.

Be mindful in public places

You may take a laptop, a tablet, an iPad, a smart phone or any other number of devices to public places and connect to the internet using them. You may even use a computer offered by the establishment, such as one in a hotel lobby. That's generally okay, and for the most part you're probably safe doing so provided you're careful. However, you should be mindful in public places, and here are a few tips.

- Don't make purchases in public places, by phone or over the internet. Someone could be listening or watching.
- If you use a public computer, be careful to tell websites *not* to remember your password.
- When connecting to a public network from one of your own devices, when prompted regarding the network type, choose Public.

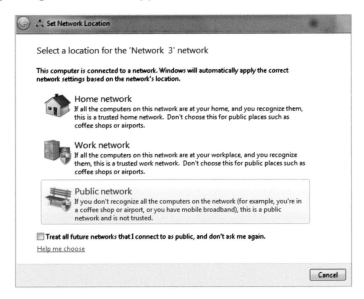

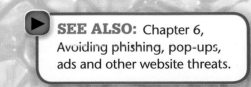

SEE ALSO: Chapter 6, Avoiding phishing, pop-ups, ads and other website threats.

- If possible, when using a public computer, start an 'InPrivate' browsing session on Windows computers. It's also a good idea to delete your browsing history.

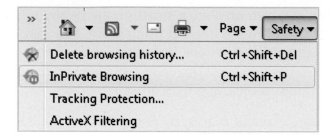

2 Fighting against viruses, adware and malware

Introduction

In the first chapter you learned the basics for staying safe on the internet. You learned to protect your devices with passwords, identify common email scams, and to refrain, when possible, from opening email attachments. You also learned that it's important to install antivirus software. That was only a brief introduction, though. In this chapter you'll delve further into one of these areas, avoiding viruses and similar online threats.

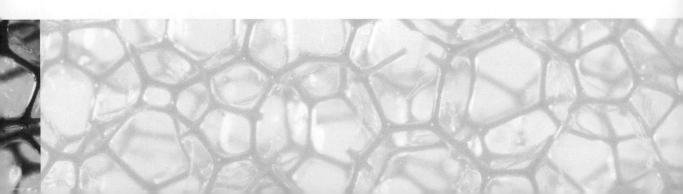

Identify the threats

Some people and companies create harmful computer code so that they can obtain personal information, steal your identity, take control of your computer or cause you to buy a product (often by coercing you into it). They may also simply want to show off their 'talents' by causing your computer harm. The common internet threats that hackers create and use that may affect you are outlined here:

- Viruses — Computer code that can replicate itself and spread from computer to computer, kind of like a cold virus that spreads from person to person. The computer virus can spread over the internet, via email, through a USB drive, CD, or DVD, and even over a network. You should install software to protect against viruses and similar threats.

- Adware — Software that plays, displays, or downloads advertisements to your computer, which are often offered as 'pop-ups' when surfing the web. Some adware may contain spyware or software that compromises your privacy.

- Spyware — Small bits of computer code that is installed on your computer without your knowledge for the purpose of collecting information about the web sites you visit, what you buy, who you are, and other personal information.

WHAT DOES THIS MEAN?
Hackers: are people who create viruses, adware, spyware, etc. in order to 'hack into' your computer without your knowledge.

 ALERT: There are other kinds of internet threats including Trojan viruses, worms, rootkits and various forms of malware.

 DID YOU KNOW?
Viruses can arrive in instant messages too.

Know who not to trust

You know that human cold viruses can be spread through physical contact and by touching shared surfaces (like doorknobs). You can lessen your chances of getting the virus if you keep your distance from the infected person and avoid touching anything they've handled. If you knew where you were most likely to pick up computer viruses, adware and spyware, you could avoid those places and lessen your chances of becoming infected.

Here are some of the places on the internet you should avoid:

- Any website that offers pornographic material.
- File sharing websites like Napster or Limewire, where people share files that aren't monitored.
- Anything with 'torrent' in the name.
- Any pop-up advertisement. In the best case scenario you'll be taken to a website you probably don't want to visit; at worst, a virus will be installed onto your computer.
- Any ad or sponsored results in a list of search results.
- Add-ons that come with software you download. Often when you opt to download a safe and trusted program, you'll be prompted also to download a new web browser or file reader.
- Free software scans and free virus scans. Most will put a fake or real virus on your computer and want you to buy their product to remove it.
- Even when downloading from a website you trust, opt out of special offers and email alerts. If you know you have never signed up, then if you do happen to get an email from a legitimate company, you know to be suspicious.

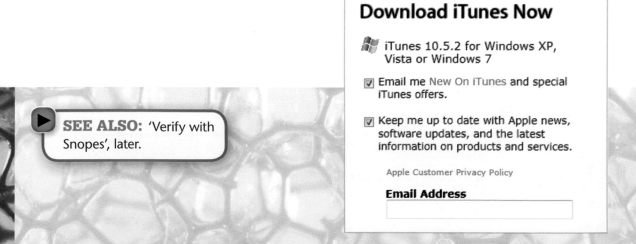

SEE ALSO: 'Verify with Snopes', later.

Download iTunes Now

iTunes 10.5.2 for Windows XP, Vista or Windows 7

☑ Email me New On iTunes and special iTunes offers.

☑ Keep me up to date with Apple news, software updates, and the latest information on products and services.

Apple Customer Privacy Policy

Email Address

Enable a firewall

Windows computers and Apple computers both offer a firewall. It should be enabled. If you get security software later that also offers a firewall, use it instead. Don't run two firewalls.

1 On a Windows computer, click Start and click Control Panel.

2 Locate or search for Windows Firewall.

3 Click Windows Firewall.

4 Verify the Firewall is turned on.

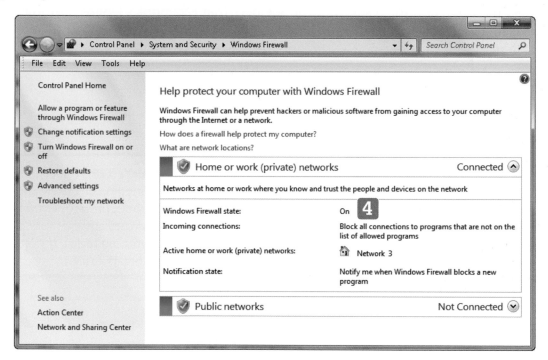

WHAT DOES THIS MEAN?

Firewall: A firewall is software that checks incoming and outgoing data to see if it's from a trusted source. It blocks data it knows is harmful.

 HOT TIP: You will have to enable specific firewall settings so that programs that need to pass through it won't get blocked. You'll be prompted to let iTunes data through, as well as data for GoogleTalk, Safari, Windows Live Messenger, and so on.

Verify with Snopes

If you're ever in doubt about the legitimacy of a video, email or internet rumour, or if you think what you're about to click may be a virus or malware, consult Snopes.com. Search the website for what you've encountered. You'll be able to discern quickly if the item is a threat or not.

1 From any web browser, navigate to www.snopes.com.

2 If you want to search for something specific, type it in the Search window.

3 Browse the results, and click any result to read.

4 Read the claim and the result. You can see here that Facebook's Dislike button is indeed a virus.

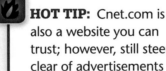

⚠ ALERT: Don't click any video or ad, or forward any email rumour until you've verified it's safe (or true) on Snopes.com.

🔥 HOT TIP: Cnet.com is also a website you can trust; however, still steer clear of advertisements and don't run any free virus scans!

🔥 HOT TIP: You can browse Snopes.com safely and learn about previous email hoaxes, viruses and malware, and you can review the latest threats easily.

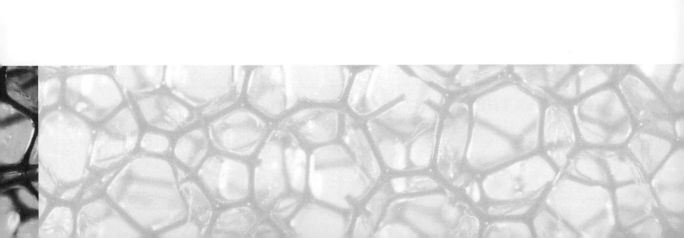

Learn the signs and symptoms of infection

A computer infected with a virus or malware often shows symptoms. The computer may run very slowly for instance, or there may be pop-ups on the screen. Odd error messages may appear, and those messages may have misspellings in them. Here are a few other signs and symptoms.

- The computer stops responding, locks up or continually restarts.
- Applications, data and drives aren't accessible.
- Files have been renamed.
- You can only visit one website or can't get online at all.
- Programs and data disappear.
- New icons appear on the desktop.
- You can't open your security (protective) software.
- Your firewall has been turned off and you can't turn it back on.

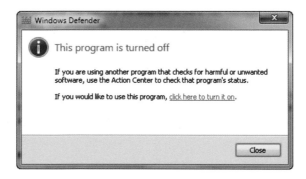

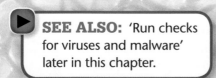 **SEE ALSO:** 'Run checks for viruses and malware' later in this chapter.

HOT TIP: The best way to avoid viruses and malware, besides installing and running trusted security software, is to avoid dangerous or seedy places on the internet.

Learn how to be safe on Facebook

If you use Facebook, and over 800 million people do, be very careful what you click or share. The video you want to watch could be a virus, the post a scam or the game riddled with ads. You can learn how to be safe on Facebook by taking the Facebook Security Quiz.

1 Log in to Facebook.

2 Visit the Facebook Security page at https://www.facebook.com/security.

3 Click Security Quiz in the left pane.

4 Click Take the Quiz.

5 When you finish, it's safe to share your new badge!

Joli Ballew

I earned a badge by testing my knowledge with the Stop. Think. Connect. Security Quiz.

Do your part to make the Internet safer and more secure by taking the quiz yourself.

Like · Comment · 10 seconds ago via Security Quiz

ALERT: There are several Facebook security pages available; you want the 'real' one. To be sure you're visiting the page associated with Facebook, type https://www.facebook.com/security in the address bar of your web browser.

HOT TIP: If you're ever in doubt about any shared post, visit www.snopes.com. Search for the name of the shared post and discover whether it's a virus or a hoax before clicking.

Obtain security software

No matter how careful you are about the email you open, the websites you visit, and the Facebook links you click, your computer will still be vulnerable to viruses if you don't install security software. You can buy software from well-known manufacturers or you can opt for trusted, proven, free software. If you're going to buy software, and you have access to a retail store, buy it there; it's just safer and it's hard to go wrong.

1 Free security software: one good, free security program is Microsoft Security Essentials. You can download it from www.windows.microsoft.com/mse, and it will start to install automatically. Click Download to get started.

2 Well-known security software: several companies produce security software and the most well-known include Norton, McAfee and Kaspersky. Unless you read a review of another security software product on a trusted site like www.cnet.com, avoid other companies.

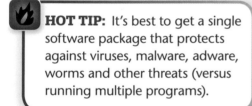

HOT TIP: It's best to get a single software package that protects against viruses, malware, adware, worms and other threats (versus running multiple programs).

HOT TIP: Another free software package is AVG Free, available at www.free.avg.com. If you opt for this, make sure you're vigilant to get the free version and aren't tricked into paying!

ALERT: In most instances, downloaded security software will start to install automatically, and all you have to do is follow the prompts to complete the installation. If it does not, refer to the next section, 'Install security software'.

ALERT: If you are worried about downloading programs online, or if you want a physical CD that contains the software you're purchasing, make the purchase from a retail store.

Install security software

After you've obtained the security software you want, you must install it. You start an installation from an installation prompt that appears when you insert a CD or DVD, or by browsing to the setup or installation file manually (such as in the case of downloaded software that does not immediately begin to install).

1 To install software from a CD or DVD:

   a Insert the CD or DVD. If prompted, choose to run or install the program.

   b If you are not prompted, navigate to the CD or DVD drive. On a Windows computer, click Start and Computer (or My Computer).

   c Double-click the drive that holds the CD or DVD.

   d Skip to step 3.

2 To install software you've downloaded:

   a Make sure you've clicked Download on the web page and that the program is saved to your computer's hard drive.

   b Locate the installation file.

3 Double-click the installation file. Here, that's a file listed in the Downloads folder. It may be an icon though, in a window.

4 Follow the prompts to complete the installation.

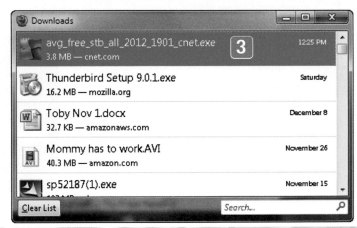

! ALERT: Be careful when downloading and installing free software. Don't also install toolbars, PDF readers and software you have to pay for.

🔥 HOT TIP: For now, accept the installation defaults. Later you can change what data gets scanned, how often the program checks for updates and so on.

Verify settings

Once security software is installed, you can configure and verify its settings. What you have access to and can change will depend on the software installed. Whatever the case though, make sure the program is set to get updates often and that it performs scans often.

1 Open your security software. You may be able to open it from the taskbar on a Windows computer.

2 Explore the tabs, and verify your computer is protected.

> 🔥 **HOT TIP:** If you're unsure of any setting, accept the default.

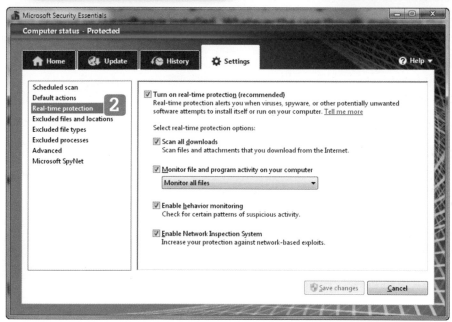

> 🔥 **HOT TIP:** If your computer is online most of the time, configure the program to check for updates (new definitions) daily.

> 🔥 **HOT TIP:** If you leave your computer turned on all night, configure scans to run daily, in the middle of the night. If not, configure scans to run on Sundays, or another day the computer isn't used much, and make sure your computer is turned on that day.

Explore Windows Defender

You should have security software installed by now, but if, for some reason, you did not heed the warnings to obtain such software, you can still count on Windows Defender to protect against some kinds of malware, specifically spyware. If you installed security software, Windows Defender is (or should be) disabled.

1 On a Windows computer, click Start.

2 Click Control Panel.

3 Locate Windows Defender. One way is to type it in the Search box.

4 If you've installed security software, you should be informed that Windows Defender is turned off. If not, turn it off.

5 If you have not installed security software, explore the Windows Defender options. (Click Home, the arrow next to Scan, History and Tools.)

6 If you see problems, and Windows Defender is your only security program, fix those problems. Here, you'd check for updates.

HOT TIP: To turn off Windows Defender, click Tools, click Options, click Real Time Protection, and disable it. Then click Automatic Scanning, and disable that. Click Save.

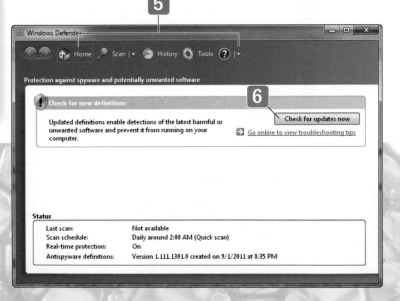

ALERT: Do not run multiple security software programs. That only confuses your computer!

Run checks for viruses and malware

If you suspect you have a security problem, you can run checks for viruses and malware. Use your security software to do this. If you don't have any security software, you'll use Windows Defender, detailed in the next section.

1 Open your security software program.

2 Verify that it's up-to-date.

3 Look for an option to scan the computer.

4 Click Scan Now, or something similar.

5 If prompted, delete or quarantine threats found.

ALERT: Windows Defender just protects against some malware, and does not protect against viruses.

ALERT: If you have a virus, your security program may not open. In this case, download and run Microsoft's Malicious Software Removal software, detailed in the last section of this chapter.

Remove spyware with Windows Defender

If Windows Defender is all you have, or if you know you have a security problem that your other security software can't resolve, you can run a scan for spyware using Windows Defender. If Windows Defender can find the problem, it can often resolve it.

1. Open Windows Defender from Control Panel or by searching for Windows Defender from the Start menu.

2. If necessary, click Check for updates now, and wait until the updates are installed.

3. Click the arrow next to scan and click Full Scan.

4. Wait while the scan completes, and if prompted, choose to quarantine the problems found.

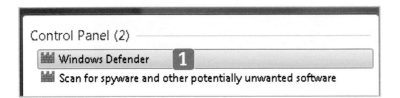

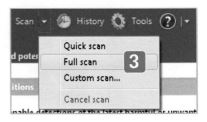

 HOT TIP: If Windows Defender is what protects you against spyware, make sure it's configured to scan your computer at least once a week.

? DID YOU KNOW?

If Windows Defender is turned off, it's probably because you have a security program that manages spyware. It may also be turned off because a virus has attacked your computer and turned it off.

WHAT DOES THIS MEAN?

Quarantine: when threats are quarantined, they are placed by themselves where they can do no harm. You can delete quarantined items if desired.

Remove viruses and malware with the Malicious Software Removal Tool

On a Windows computer, sometimes Windows Defender and/or your security software can't get rid of a computer virus, spyware or malware. Perhaps you can't access the program, you can't get online or the program runs but doesn't fix the problem. In these cases you can try Microsoft's Malicious Software Removal Tool.

1 Navigate to http://www.microsoft.com/security/pc-security/malware-removal.aspx.

2 Read what's offered, if desired, and then click Download the Tool located at the bottom of the page.

3 Click Download and be patient while the download completes.

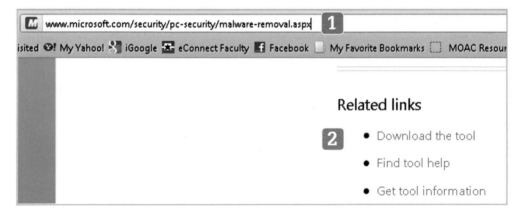

ALERT: If you can't get online to download the required program from the infected computer, you may be able to download the program and related files to another computer you own, copy the data to a CD or USB drive, and use that as a basis for running the program on the infected computer.

4 To start the installation, click Run (if it appears). If Save is the only option, or to save the installation files for use on another computer, click Save File.

5 If applicable, double-click the installation file in the Downloads list or applicable folder.

6 Complete the installation and scan as prompted, and follow any directions to rid the computer of the threat, as applicable.

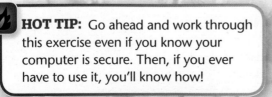

HOT TIP: Go ahead and work through this exercise even if you know your computer is secure. Then, if you ever have to use it, you'll know how!

3 Avoiding threats in email

Introduction

You will receive email that you should not open, reply to, purchase goods from or believe. The email may claim you've won a prize, that you need to update your personal information at a bank or that you're about to inherit a lot of money. These emails are often fairly easy to spot if you know what to look for, but sometimes they can be harder to distinguish from legitimate mail. Some crafty scammers will try to make a purchase from your company and then fail to pay (or payment will bounce), or ask you to send them, say $100, in exchange for a winning lottery ticket they can't cash themselves, among other things.

In this chapter you'll learn how to protect yourself from threats that will arrive in your inbox. You'll learn some common and not-so-common scams, and how to determine if the sender or the websites you're supposed to visit are valid. You'll also learn a bit about keeping potentially dangerous email out of your inbox so that you never see it, a slightly different concept than simply avoiding spam for convenience (as outlined in the next chapter).

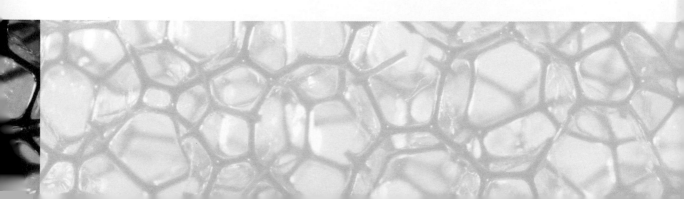

Keep your email program up to date

The company that created the program you use to get your email, such as Microsoft (Outlook or Windows Live, for instance), Mozilla (Thunderbird) or Apple (Mail), will occasionally offer updates when security issues are uncovered and resolved. It's important to get these updates to avoid known security issues.

1 Make sure your computer is set to get updates. On Windows computers, this is achieved through Windows Update.

2 Make sure any third-party email programs are set to obtain and install updates automatically.

3 If prompted to manually install an update, do so.

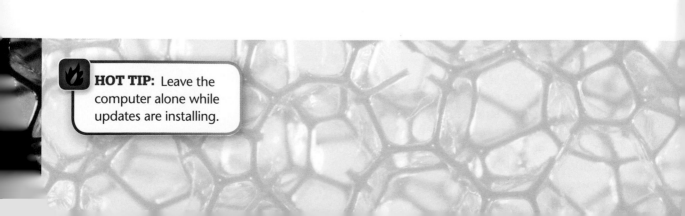

HOT TIP: Leave the computer alone while updates are installing.

Know common signs of scam emails

There are some things that are common to emails from people that are out to scam you. Misspelled words are a dead giveaway, as is bad grammar and poorly written text. You can rest assured that email from your bank won't have any typographical errors in it. Here are some additional signs.

- Someone wants you to send them money.

- You are asked to provide (for whatever reason), personally identifiable information such as a National Insurance number, user name or password.

- The email originated in Nigeria or other foreign country and/or there are a lot of capital letters in the email.

Subject **FROM UNITED STATES AMBASSADOR TO NIGERIA**

To Joli Ballew

To: undisclosed-recipients:
Subject: FROM UNITED STATES AMBASSADOR TO NIGERIA

UNITED STATES AMBASSADOR TO NIGERIA
U.S. DEPARTMENT OF STATE
BUREAU OF CONSULAR AFFAIRS
U.S AMBASSADOR TO NIGERIA
11 GARIK ROAD ABUJA

Attention beneficiary,

My name is Terence Patrick McCulley, the new United States amba
senate had confirmed my nomination on august 5th 2010 after being

- The sender claims to be royalty, a distant relative, a prison inmate looking for friendship or a young woman looking for love.

- Your email program sends the email to the Junk or Spam folder, or denotes the email with a distinct warning.

! ALERT: Never respond to emails you believe to be scams, even out of curiosity or to inconvenience the sender.

- The sender's email address is invalid or complex.

> From ELİTAŞKLAR.COM <c34kTmNtz7YtAuxTY0MIL5@konuk.net> ☆
> Subject **nurgul - sarsilarak bosalmak istiyorum**
> To joli_ballew@hotmail.com ☆
>
> **Junk Mail**
>
> ---
>
> -
> Sayin uyemiz, Bir yeni mesaj aldiniz!
> Alt kisimlarda bulunmakta olan bilgilerle siteye hesabiniza erisebilirsiniz.
>
> Email : joli_ballew@hotmail.com
> Sifre : 123456789
>
> Otomatik Giriş için Tıklayın!
>
> **ELİTAŞKLAR.COM**

- Your email program suggests the email is a scam.

> ⚠ **This message may be a scam.**
> Disable scam detection for all messages   [Ignore Warning]

? DID YOU KNOW?

Email providers keep track of the email users manually mark as 'junk', and add known spam and scam emails to a sort of 'black list'. Email that falls into this category never makes it to your inbox.

Don't talk to strangers!

Your mother told you, and you told your children and grandchildren: don't talk to strangers! The same holds true for people who email you. No matter how sincere the person who sends the email sounds, don't answer. Just hit the Delete button. Better yet, hit the Junk button. Here are some common ways scammers will try to initiate a conversation:

- They are an injured war veteran. They need money for medical supplies, a wheelchair and so on.
- They are just looking for love and companionship.
- A mother needs money for medical care to aid her sick child.
- A prison inmate only wants a pen pal.
- An illegal alien has a winning lottery ticket and needs someone to cash it.
- A sick or dying Nigerian needs help with expenses.
- A person wants to make a purchase from your company, and wants you to send the goods first and they'll pay once they get them.

Subject **THE TRUTH ABOUT YOUR FUND, CONTACT AGENT KELVIN WILLIAMS ASAP ,**

To Joli Ballew ☆

```
I am Mr. Tom Smith, I am a US citizen, 48 years Old, I reside here in New
York City  My residential address is as follows. 160 Central Park South, New
York United States, I am one of those that took part in the Compensation in
Nigeria many years ago and they refused to pay me, I had paid over $50,000
while in the US, trying to get my payment all to no avail.
```

 HOT TIP: If you see foreign text in an email's body or subject line and you do not recognise the sender, delete the email.

ALERT: Some email from strangers is very, very sad. Try not to be taken in; 99.9 per cent of the time, it's only a play for your money.

Explore the validity of the sender's name

Some senders mask the name that appears in the From: line to make the email appear as though it's from a valid source, when in reality it is not. In many email programs and browsers, the actual email address appears next to the name, as shown here. This is good, because you can tell if the email address matches the sender's name and is one you recognise. If you can't see the email address but can only see the name instead, don't do anything with the email until you're sure you know who it is from.

Start the New Year off Right with More Miles!

AAdvantage eShopping Mall <support@aadvantageeshopping.com>

Sent: Sun 1/1/2012 2:12 PM

To: joli_ballew@tx.rr.com

---

1 If you get your email from a web browser, by navigating to a web page, you may be able to see the actual email address by hovering your mouse over the name.

2 If you get your email from a program installed on your computer, hovering will probably work there too. If not, click once on the sender's name.

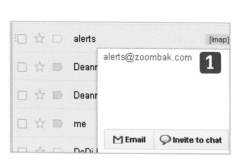

🔥 **HOT TIP:** You can often right-click the email address in the To: line to view additional options, like Properties or Edit.

❗ **ALERT:** If the email is supposed to be from, say, CitiBank, but the email address is something like CD43Dclies450@mywebaddress.com, it's not legitimate.

Hover before you click that link

It's easy for someone to create a link in an email where the name of the link is different from the actual website you'll be taken to if you click it. This means that a link's name could be the name of a legitimate company, but the website it is pointing to is something completely different. Before clicking any link, hover the mouse over it to see where the link actually goes.

1 Open any email that contains a link to a web page.

2 Hover your mouse over the link.

3 Verify that the words after *www* represents the site you really want to go to.

4 Click the link only if you know the website link is a valid one. Better yet, navigate to the site yourself, as outlined in the next section.

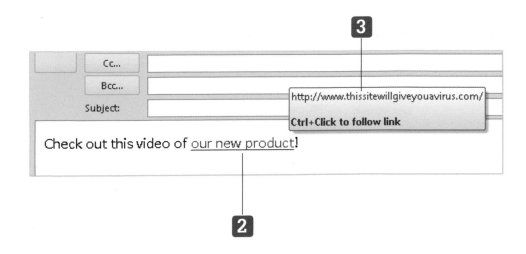

ALERT: When in doubt about a link, don't click it.

ALERT: If you want to click a link for a bank, company or well-known online site (like Microsoft or Apple), note that the words after *www* should contain the company name (www.microsoft.com, for instance). It's okay if something else follows those words though (www.microsoft.com/security).

When in doubt, visit the entity's official website

If you receive an email from a company you trust and/or have an account with, and you receive an email that asks you to reply with your personal information for 'verification' or some such thing, and you can't tell from the sender's email address or any links in the body of the email if it is a scam, you still have options. You can visit the website by typing in the address manually, and look there for information.

1 Open your web browser. This may be Safari, Firefox or Internet Explorer, for instance.

2 In the address bar, type the name of the website you'd like to visit.

3 Look around the site for a Security tab or a Help tab.

? DID YOU KNOW?

If a company, like a financial institution, needs you to update your personal information, you'll be prompted to do so when you log on to the website. You will never be asked to provide that information in an email. It's just not secure.

4 Locate information about recent email scams. Here is an example of a scam email. This email is *not* from Citibank!

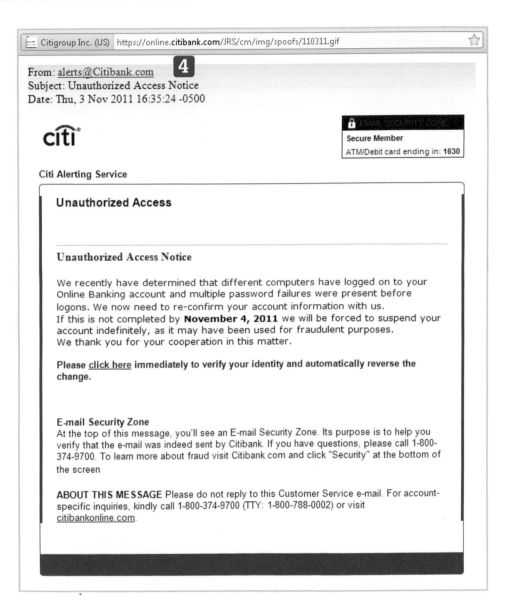

From: alerts@Citibank.com **4**
Subject: Unauthorized Access Notice
Date: Thu, 3 Nov 2011 16:35:24 -0500

citi®

🔒 EMAIL SECURITY ZONE
Secure Member
ATM/Debit card ending in: **1630**

Citi Alerting Service

Unauthorized Access

Unauthorized Access Notice

We recently have determined that different computers have logged on to your Online Banking account and multiple password failures were present before logons. We now need to re-confirm your account information with us.
If this is not completed by **November 4, 2011** we will be forced to suspend your account indefinitely, as it may have been used for fraudulent purposes.
We thank you for your cooperation in this matter.

Please click here immediately to verify your identity and automatically reverse the change.

E-mail Security Zone
At the top of this message, you'll see an E-mail Security Zone. Its purpose is to help you verify that the e-mail was indeed sent by Citibank. If you have questions, please call 1-800-374-9700. To learn more about fraud visit Citibank.com and click "Security" at the bottom of the screen

ABOUT THIS MESSAGE Please do not reply to this Customer Service e-mail. For account-specific inquiries, kindly call 1-800-374-9700 (TTY: 1-800-788-0002) or visit citibankonline.com.

 HOT TIP: Always hover the mouse or click the sender's address to see who it's from.

 ALERT: Always hover the mouse over a link before clicking it. If the link claims to go to www.citi.com but instead goes to www.123x7z.ripyouoff.com, don't click it.

Triple check before opening an attachment

You already know that attachments that come with emails can contain viruses and other problematic computer code. And since viruses can replicate themselves and spread through email, it's possible to get a virus from an email sent by someone you know. First and foremost, make sure your security software is set to scan all attachments, as shown here.

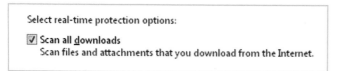

Select real-time protection options:

☑ Scan all downloads
Scan files and attachments that you download from the Internet.

Then, review these additional tips to stay safe.

- Understand that it's perfectly OK to reply to the sender and ask if they meant to send the email attachment, and if they believe it's safe to open.
- Hover your mouse over the attachment to see what kind of file it is. It's safe to open PDF files, pictures and most documents, but don't open anything that is an EXE, BAT, COM, PIF or SCR.

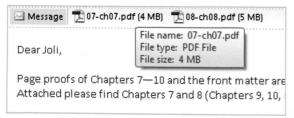

✉ Message 📄 07-ch07.pdf (4 MB) 📄 08-ch08.pdf (5 MB)

File name: 07-ch07.pdf
File type: PDF File
File size: 4 MB

Dear Joli,

Page proofs of Chapters 7—10 and the front matter are
Attached please find Chapters 7 and 8 (Chapters 9, 10,

- Beware of files that have an 'm' in their name, like .docm, .xlsm and so on. These are office files that contain macros. Macros are computer code, and can be unsafe.

 DID YOU KNOW?
The name of the attachment may appear to be safe, such as *pictureofme.jpg*, but when you hover over it, you may find it's really *pictureofme.jpg.exe*. Clicking that would be bad indeed!

WHAT DOES THIS MEAN?
.exe: files that end in .exe are executable files, and clicking them causes a program installation to begin.

 HOT TIP: You can configure security software to scan attachments for viruses before they are opened.

Configure a junk email filter

If you keep junk mail from getting into your inbox, you'll certainly be much less likely to fall for a scam you see there. Thus, one of the ways to protect yourself is to set a junk email filter. How you go about this depends how you get your email.

- If you use Microsoft Outlook, from the Home tab, click the arrow under Junk, and click Junk E-Mail options to configure settings.
- If you use Mozilla Thunderbird, click Tools, Options and the Junk tab.
- If you use Windows Live Mail, from the Home tab, click the arrow under Junk, and click Safety Options, as shown here.

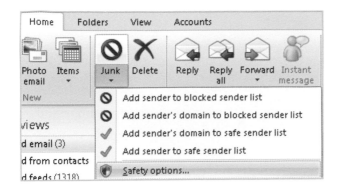

- If you use Apple Mail, go to Mail, Preferences and then Junk Mail.
- If you use a web-based method then visit the web page where you get your email, and search for junk mail filtering options.

Preventing junk email

Filters and reporting

Safe and blocked senders

Block unwanted senders

When you get email from a person or company you do not want to receive mail from, you can block the sender before deleting the email, and the next time an email arrives from that exact email address it will go directly to the Junk or Spam folder, Deleted Items folder or some other trash folder.

- Look for the Block Sender button on the Home tab or near the Junk mail option.
- Look for the Block Sender option under the Junk option.
- If you see no way to block a sender, mark the email as Junk or a Phishing message.

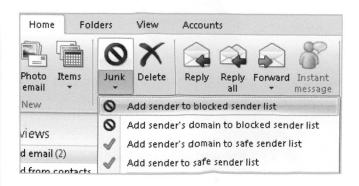

? DID YOU KNOW?

Blocking senders is not the best way to handle unwanted email that gets through your junk email filter (but it won't hurt), because many scammers use a different email address every time they email you. However, it is a good way to block email from companies, although getting off mailing lists is even better.

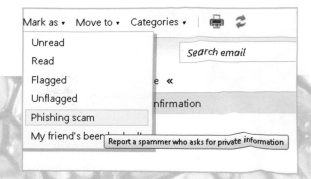

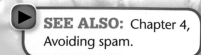 **SEE ALSO:** Chapter 4, Avoiding spam.

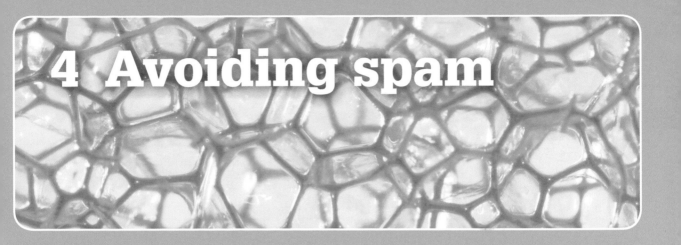

4 Avoiding spam

Introduction

Everyone gets some junk email. How much you get now and how much you'll get in the future depends a lot on how well you protect your primary email address. To reduce the spam you get now, unsubscribe from valid mailing lists, social networking updates, shopping websites and other legitimate entities. This can minimise the mail you get by half or more!

To minimise the amount of spam you'll get in the future, obtain a secondary email address. Use this address to make purchases online, and to log on to websites to make comments on news stories, get personalised pages and the like. Beyond this though, with the right software you can block entire domains, block email from foreign countries and increase the strength of your Spam filter, among other things.

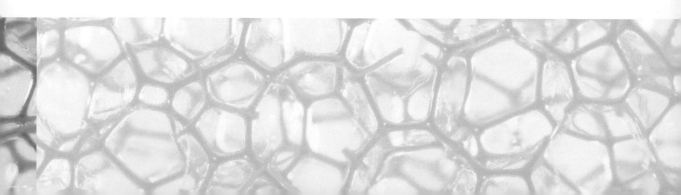

Don't share your primary email address

There are a lot of people that want to know your primary email address. However, you should only share it (at least from now on), with people and companies you really do want to hear from regularly and who need a reliable way to contact you. If you aren't sure what address someone has used to send you mail, refer to the To: line in any email you receive. Here are a few people and entities you can share your personal email with:

- family and friends; doctors and lawyers
- clients and business partners (unless you have a separate business account)
- government departments
- banks and financial institutions
- insurance providers
- brokers and independent financial advisers.

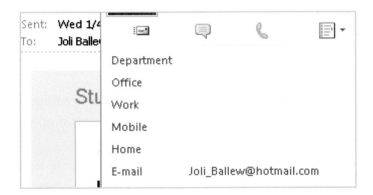

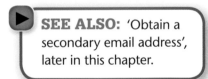

SEE ALSO: 'Obtain a secondary email address', later in this chapter.

WHAT DOES THIS MEAN?

Primary email address: this is generally the address you use when you communicate with family and friends, or doctors and lawyers. It's the address you check daily.

Tell your friends and family not to share your email address

Protecting your email address and keeping it out of the hands of spammers requires you to be careful about whom you share the address with. However, there's more to it than that. You have to tell others not to share it too. For instance, a caring grandchild could create a birthday card for you on a website, and then give the website your email address so they can send it!

- Tell contacts if they want to share a story on a web page to copy the link and email it to you personally and refrain from using a tool like the one shown here.

- Make sure contacts understand you don't want to receive invitations or greetings cards from party planning websites. (You can tell them you simply prefer old-fashioned invitations!)
- Understand that it's perfectly alright to tell people that you are trying to keep your email address private and to expect them to respect your wishes.

 DID YOU KNOW?

Some websites that provide services like those that offer a way to send out party invitations via email, create greeting cards or share data on their site with others, may do so for the sole purpose of mining (and selling) email addresses for a profit.

HOT TIP: Create a secondary email address and give that address to grandchildren and others you think may not be able to keep your personal email address private.

Unsubscribe from legitimate mailing lists

The next time you receive an email from Amazon.com touting this week's special deals, remember that you probably signed up to receive it! When you get an email from your favourite airline informing you of the newest getaway holiday, the same is probably true. When a legitimate company is involved, it's possible to unsubscribe safely.

1 Scroll to the bottom of the email.

2 Look for an option to unsubscribe or opt out.

3 Click that option.

4 Perform the necessary steps to be removed.

Amazon.com Communications

We want to stay in touch, but only in ways that you find h

You have already set your preference to only receive esser your communication preferences here.

The e-mail you received pertained to the categories below. e-mail notifications from these categories. If you unsubscri

☑ **Books**

[Unsubscribe] — **3**

You may also unsubscribe from all Amazon marketing commu transactional e-mail (transactional e-mail includes message: AmazonLocal and Amazon.com Delivers subscriptions.

[Unsubscribe from all] — **3**

 ALERT: Never click Unsubscribe, Opt out or similar options from a company or person you do not know or have never done business with. This will increase the amount of spam you get not lessen it!

 ALERT: Before you unsubscribe by clicking a link in the body of an email, use all of the techniques outlined in Chapter 3 to verify the email is actually from the company it claims to be. If you are the least bit unsure, unsubscribe directly from the company's website.

HOT TIP: Although you should not click the Unsubscribe or Opt out button in most emails, it's okay to do so when a legitimate company that you do business with is involved.

Unsubscribe from unwanted social networking email

If you are a member of Facebook, LinkedIn or a similar social networking site, you are likely to get email. You can reduce or eliminate much (if not all) of this email by changing your preferences at the related website. In this example, Facebook is used, but other websites are configured similarly.

1 Log on to www.facebook.com.

2 Click the arrow beside Home, and click Account Settings.

3 In the left pane, click Notifications.

4 Next to Facebook, click Edit.

5 Select and deselect as desired. A tick means you'll receive email.

6 Continue to modify all of the other options including but not limited to Photos, Groups, Pages, Events, etc.

HOT TIP: If you don't see the option to change email notifications under Account Settings in the social network you use, try Privacy Settings, Notifications, Email Preferences or other options.

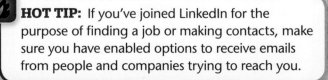
HOT TIP: If you've joined LinkedIn for the purpose of finding a job or making contacts, make sure you have enabled options to receive emails from people and companies trying to reach you.

Know what to do when you can't click Unsubscribe

You learned earlier that it's generally safe to unsubscribe to email (from the body of the email) if it's a legitimate company you do business with. However, for email from unknown entities or those you've never done business with, that's not an option. Additionally, some email that comes from legitimate companies will not provide an option to stop receiving email from them. In these cases you can often visit the website to opt out.

E-mail administration
If you no longer wish to receive this e-mail, please update your *In The Vanguard* newsletter preferences on vanguard.com. Please do not reply to this message to opt out.

- If the email is from a company you do not do business with or do not recognise, use the option to block the sender if available. Mark the mail as junk mail or spam.

- If the email is from a company you recognise as legitimate, visit the company's website and look for an option to stop receiving emails from it.

- If neither of these options stops email from the company, refer to the next section, 'Block email from entire domains'.

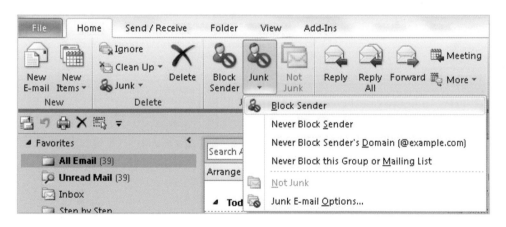

ALERT: Unsubscribe options in emails from companies you don't recognise are probably there to obtain and then sell your email address, making the spam problem worse!

SEE ALSO: 'Block unwanted senders' in Chapter 3.

Block email from entire domains

Sometimes, no matter how many steps you take, you simply can't stop emails from a company from coming. You may have blocked specific addresses and marked the emails as junk, but other emails with different address from the same company still arrive. When this happens you can often block all email from that company by blocking the company's *domain*. The way to achieve this depends on how you get your email though, so these are generic steps.

1 Open the email program you use to get your email.

2 Locate the Junk email options.

3 Locate the Blocked Senders tab.

4 Click Add.

5 Type the domain name to block.

6 Click OK as required.

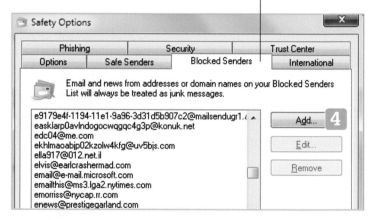

 HOT TIP: To figure out the domain name of a company from an email address, look at the last few entries of the sender's email address, specifically what comes after the @ sign. (The domain to block from the email address xyz123. TR.f@IwillSpamYou.com is IwillSpamYou.com.)

WHAT DOES THIS MEAN?

Domain: this is a specific kind of network, and the domain name is often an incarnation of the company name. For instance, Microsoft's domain name is Microsoft.com.

Block email from foreign countries

Domain names are often related to companies, like Saab.com, but top-level domain names exist that represent entire countries. You can block email from a country by blocking its top-level domain. The way you do this varies depending on the email program you use to get your email. These are generic steps.

1 Open the email program you use to get your email.

2 Locate the Junk email options.

3 Locate the International tab. (You can also block countries using the Block Senders tab.)

4 Opt to block specific top-level domains as desired.

5 Click OK as required.

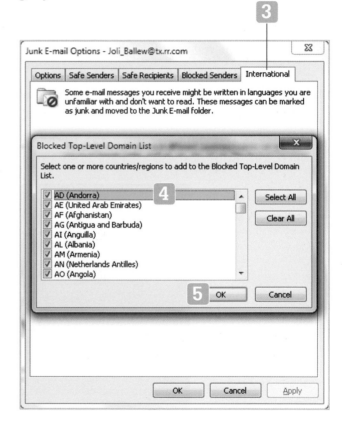

HOT TIP: If you can't access an International tab you can block top-level domains from the Block Senders tab. Top-level domains are represented with an abbreviation such as AE (United Arab Emirates) and AL (Albania).

DID YOU KNOW?
With certain email programs you can also block specific character sets (called **encodings**).

Obtain a secondary email address

Because you only want to share your primary email with people you know, and because you will still need an email address for creating user accounts, logging on to websites, and placing orders with online companies, it's important to obtain a second email address.

- Gmail: visit www.gmail.com for a free, web-based, email account from Google. It's easy to set up a Gmail account on any device, including a Kindle Fire, shown below.
- Yahoo!: visit www.yahoo.com for a free, web-based, email account from Yahoo!. Yahoo may be more difficult to set up with some email programs, although it should be compatible on most mobile devices.
- AOL: visit www.aol.com for a free, web-based email account from AOL. If you use AIM, this is a good option, otherwise, go with Gmail.
- Hotmail or Live: visit www.live.com to obtain a free web-based email address from Microsoft. Both of these are easy to set up in most email programs and devices.

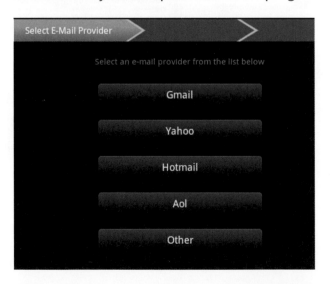

HOT TIP: If you start to get a lot of spam to a secondary email address, you can simply stop using it and get another.

? DID YOU KNOW?

Get your secondary email address from a provider such as Google, Yahoo! or AOL instead of one from your internet service provider. In general, those addresses are easier to set up and access on other devices.

Know when to use your secondary email address

You learned at the beginning of this chapter who you should share your personal, primary email address with. You should use your secondary email address with everyone else. Here are a few of the places where you should *definitely* use your secondary address:

- online stores
- news and weather websites you want to log in to
- newsgroups, mailing lists and newsletters
- social networking websites
- any website or person you believe may share your address with others.

Avoid unwittingly signing up for unwanted email

You should always use a secondary email address when making online purchases and you should only make purchases from legitimate companies. Beyond the obvious security issues with buying from fly-by-night companies, often such companies will send you daily or weekly email after the purchase and offer no way to opt out. However, even legitimate companies will prompt you to sign up for email alerts:

- when you create a user account
- during the checkout process
- before you download something
- when you apply for a credit card
- when you open a bank account.

> ☑ Yes, I would like to receive occasional CNN member updates about new features and special offers.
>
> CNN will use the information you submit in a manner consistent with our Privacy Policy. By clicking on "sign up" you agree with CNN's Terms of Service and Privacy Policy and consent to the collection, storage and use of this information in the U.S. subject to U.S. laws and regulations. (learn more)
>
> **SIGN UP**

 HOT TIP: Websites know it's easy for you to click Next or Continue when signing up for a user account or making a purchase (without reading the fine print first), but often this is where the email sign-up options are listed.

 HOT TIP: Not all companies require you to create a user account to make a purchase. Many offer options to make a purchase as a guest. This often eliminates many of the steps required to make the purchase, and can reduce the amount of prompts to sign up for email alerts and newsletters.

Opt not to receive email from third parties

You may want to receive email from a specific company. For instance, you may want to receive information from British Airways about last minute travel deals or from Amazon about weekly specials. You may want to hear about specials from Apple when you download iTunes. When you opt in to these types of emails though, you're often also prompted to opt in to receive additional email, sometimes from third parties.

1 If you opt in to receive emails, read the options carefully.

2 Deselect any option to receive email from third parties.

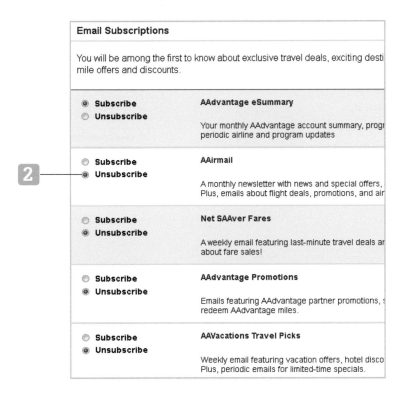

Email Subscriptions

You will be among the first to know about exclusive travel deals, exciting desti mile offers and discounts.

⦿ Subscribe ○ Unsubscribe	**AAdvantage eSummary** Your monthly AAdvantage account summary, progr periodic airline and program updates
○ Subscribe ⦿ Unsubscribe	**AAirmail** A monthly newsletter with news and special offers, Plus, emails about flight deals, promotions, and air
○ Subscribe ⦿ Unsubscribe	**Net SAAver Fares** A weekly email featuring last-minute travel deals ar about fare sales!
○ Subscribe ⦿ Unsubscribe	**AAdvantage Promotions** Emails featuring AAdvantage partner promotions, redeem AAdvantage miles.
○ Subscribe ⦿ Unsubscribe	**AAVacations Travel Picks** Weekly email featuring vacation offers, hotel disco Plus, periodic emails for limited-time specials.

! ALERT: Unless you're positive you want to receive emails from a company or its subsidiaries, always be vigilant and opt out of receiving emails. It's so easy to simply click OK, Next, Continue, Sign up, and the like.

 HOT TIP: You can unsubscribe from some emails while receiving others from a legitimate company's website.

Opt not to download images in emails

Images you receive in unwanted emails have a little beacon (of sorts) in them that alerts the spammer that it's been received. Once spammers know that they have a working email address, they'll keep sending email to it. They may even sell the email address to others. Most email programs offer an option to prevent this, unless you specifically say you trust the sender. This can help control spam.

1 If you've ever seen a message like the one shown below, the option to block images in email is already enabled.

2 If you've never seen this message and images in emails always appear, look for the option to enable the feature. Look for this option under Safety Options, Security Options or something similar.

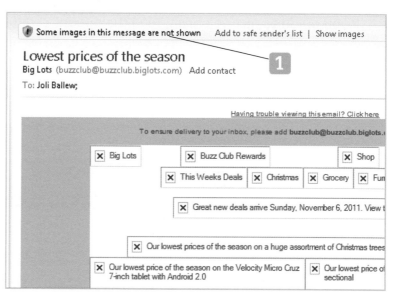

? DID YOU KNOW?
Senders you approve will be added to your Safe Senders list.

HOT TIP: If you receive an email you want to exempt from the rule, label the email as Not Junk, Safe or Always allow the sender, as applicable, to your email program.

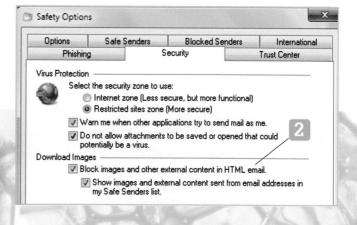

Set a stronger spam filter

All email programs and email websites offer a way to control spam, and offer options to change how strict the filter is. Windows Live Mail offers what's shown below, for instance. If you're still getting too much spam, increase the setting. Here are a few things to remember when you change the junk mail setting.

- The highest setting may only allow email from people on your Safe Senders list to arrive. This is often too strict a setting.
- A high setting will send some legitimate mail to the junk or spam folder, so you'll have to check it often.
- A medium setting is a good choice for most people, and most spam is rejected, while most legitimate mail arrives safely.
- A low setting doesn't block much junk mail at all.

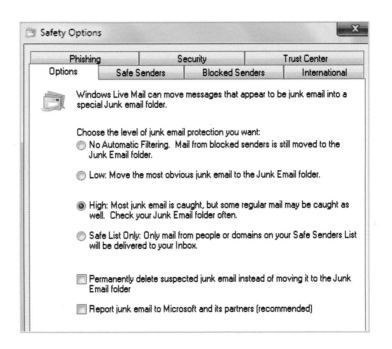

? DID YOU KNOW?

Some email programs don't offer many options at all, other than turning on the junk email filter.

- If available, choose to automatically move items you mark as Junk to the Trash or Junk folder.
- Don't opt to automatically delete email that is deemed junk; it may not be.

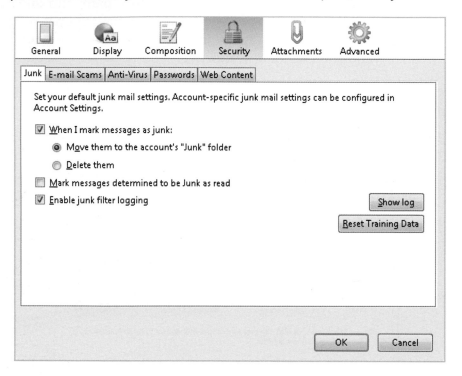

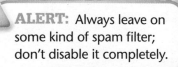 **ALERT:** Always leave on some kind of spam filter; don't disable it completely.

 HOT TIP: Mark unwanted mail as junk mail to train the junk filter with your preferences.

5 Using alternative web browsers

Introduction

You use a web browser to access web pages on the internet. Microsoft's Internet Explorer is the most-used web browser, but others are catching up quickly. Mozilla's Firefox is running a fairly close second, and Google's Chrome is third. Apple's Safari is fourth, with a few others bringing up the rear. Keep in mind that these are browsers you install and use on computers; you use other kinds of web browsers on tablets, smartphones and the like.

You can choose to use just about any web browsers on just about any computer. In most cases, it doesn't matter who made the computer or if it runs a version of Windows or something from Apple. Every browser does basically the same thing too, no matter which one you choose. All offer options to visit any web page, create bookmarks, configure security settings, block pop-ups and so on. The main differences among browsers are their interfaces, access to features and how you download and access downloaded files.

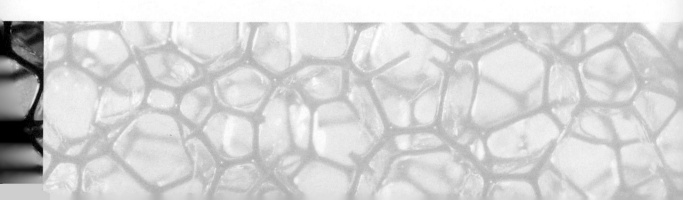

Explore Internet Explorer 9

Internet Explorer has been around for more than 15 years, and Internet Explorer 9 (IE9) is the most recent incarnation of Microsoft's popular web browser. Like other web browsers it can be configured to have a streamlined look or you can opt to show menus and toolbars. If you're new to IE9, here are a few things to explore.

1 You can right-click the very top of the interface to access the options to add built-in toolbars. Select the toolbars you want to have access to all the time.

2 If you have IE installed, show the Menu bar and then click each item on it (File, Edit, View and so on) to see what's available under them.

3 As with other browsers you can click the empty 'tab' to the right of the open tabs to open a new, blank, web page window.

HOT TIP: When you need access to the Menu bar but don't want to show the Menu bar all the time, tap the Alt key on the keyboard.

? DID YOU KNOW?

The general assumption about the various browsers is that hackers target Internet Explorer more often than the others because more people use it. They then assume that Internet Explorer must be the least secure. This may have been partly true in the past, but with the market share evening out and hackers becoming more savvy, other browsers are just as vulnerable to attacks.

? DID YOU KNOW?

IE9 does not offer a search window. This means you'll have to either search from the address bar or navigate to a site like www.google.com first.

Explore Firefox

Firefox is another web browser that is quite popular. It has about a quarter of the market share. Like other web browsers, the various toolbars and features run across the top of the window and you can show or hide them.

- A search window is built right in for easy searching, and you can add or use specific search engines easily.

- You can tap the F11 key on the keyboard to view Firefox in full screen mode. (Press F11 again to revert.)
- It's easy to access pages you've recently visited from the History menu.
- You can bookmark a page by clicking the star at the end of the Address window.
- You can easily open a new web page by clicking the + sign to the right of already open web pages.

? DID YOU KNOW?

The toolbars you see here aren't shown by default. You'll learn how to add toolbars later in this chapter.

? DID YOU KNOW?

You can use the key combination Ctrl and the Plus sign to zoom in on a web page quickly. They both have to be pressed simultaneously.

Explore Chrome

Chrome is another option for surfing the web. Like other web browsers, its goal is to make more of the screen available for web content, and less that's cluttered with toolbars and menus. This is how Chrome looks when you first install it.

- With Chrome, you can search the web from the Address bar.
- If you sign in to Chrome, your bookmarks, history and other web settings will be available no matter what computer you use.
- You can access the Chrome Web Store, where you can download and add applications such as Google Books, shown here.

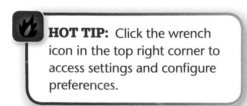

HOT TIP: Click the wrench icon in the top right corner to access settings and configure preferences.

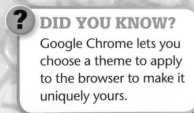

DID YOU KNOW?

Google Chrome lets you choose a theme to apply to the browser to make it uniquely yours.

Explore Safari

Safari isn't just for Apple computers; you can install Safari on your Windows computer too. Safari has a nice 'Top Sites' feature that is active by default. It's a clever way to access your favourite websites quickly.

1 To enable Safari's Top Sites, click the Top Sites button (it's selected here). Then click any website to navigate there.

2 Search for anything using the built-in Search window.

3 Shift + click on any link in a web page to add it to Safari's unique reading list.

4 Access the reading list by clicking the icon that looks like a pair of reading glasses.

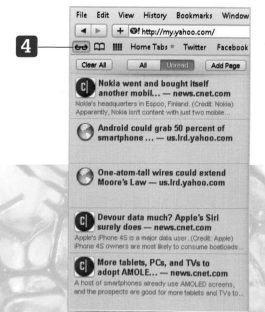

ALERT: The first time you use a new web browser, it will seem lightning fast. That's because there is no 'baggage' yet. All browsers slow down over time due to add-ons and other factors.

HOT TIP: To hide or show interface elements, click the View tab. If you hide the Menu bar though, you'll have to tap Alt on the keyboard to show it again.

Locate browser installation files

If you think you'd like to try one of these browsers, you have to locate the installation files. The installation files for all four browsers introduced so far are available from the respective company's website.

- Get Internet Explorer 9 at *www.microsoft.com/IE9.*
- Get Firefox at www.mozilla.org.
- Get Chrome at www.google.com/chrome.
- Get Safari at www.apple.com/safari.

? DID YOU KNOW?
Because web browsers are easy to download and install, and just as easy to uninstall, feel free to try out any browser you like!

! ALERT: Always download these browsers from the websites listed here, and provided by the company that produced them.

HOT TIP: If prompted to install add-ons, like Adobe Reader, a toolbar or other items, decline for now. You can always add them later if you want.

Download and install a browser

Once you've located the installation files for a browser you want to install, you have to download those files and then run the installation program. How you do this depends on the browser you're currently using. Once you've accessed the installation files, you may have to work through the installation process by clicking OK, Next, Continue or the like.

- If you are using the latest version of Internet Explorer to download files, you'll have to be patient for the download to become available, and then look for the Run option at the bottom of the IE window.

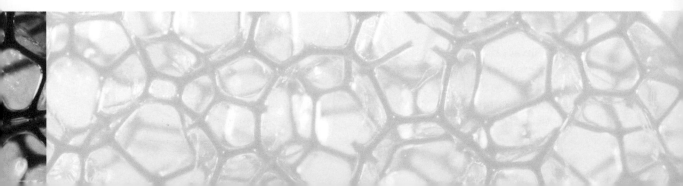

- If you're using Firefox, you'll have to click Save File when prompted, and then look for the installation files in the Downloads window.

- If you're using Safari, click Run.

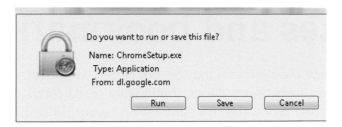

Do you want to run or save this file?

Name: ChromeSetup.exe
Type: Application
From: dl.google.com

[Run]   [Save]   [Cancel]

- If you're running Chrome, you may have to click Keep if Chrome thinks the file is dangerous, and then click the installation file that appears at the bottom of the Chrome window to start the installation process.

 HOT TIP: There's really no reason to save a new browser's installation files. Thus, if Run is an option after you've downloaded the files, click it instead of Save.

! ALERT: If you download and install a web browser and later decide you don't like it, uninstall it. You do not want to bog down your computer with unwanted files and programs.

Import and access existing favourites and bookmarks

When you install a new browser, you may be prompted to import your favourites or bookmarks from your existing browser. If you want to do this, simply click the appropriate option when prompted. If your existing favourites or bookmarks are unorganised or if you do not want to import them, click No. Once you've imported bookmarks or favourites, you'll have to learn how to access them.

1 Depending on the browser, look under the Bookmarks or Favorites tab for your list of websites. If you can't see this tab, tap the Alt key on the keyboard.

2 Click Organize bookmarks or Organize favorites to delete or group existing bookmarks easily.

3 Chrome's bookmarks are located under the wrench icon.

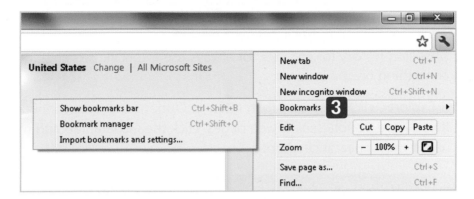

4 When creating new bookmarks, consider saving the ones you use every day to the Bookmarks bar or Favorites bar, if applicable.

WHAT DOES THIS MEAN?

Bookmarks and favourites: these are terms used to describe the web pages you specifically mark as those you'd like to visit again. Some browsers come with bookmarks and favourites already created.

Access and configure settings

All web browsers offer a way to configure preferences and settings. You may want to delete your browsing history for instance, or always use a specific search engine when researching something on the internet.

● In Internet Explorer, click Tools and then Internet Options to locate configuration settings. If you have trouble seeing web pages, click the General tab and make changes under the Appearance options.

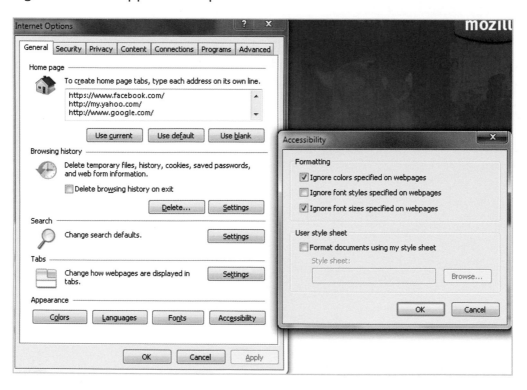

- In Firefox, click Tools and then Options. If you're worried about privacy, from the Privacy tab select Tell websites I do not want to be tracked.
- In Chrome, click the wrench icon and click Options. To set a default zoom setting, click Under the Hood, and then select a Page zoom setting.

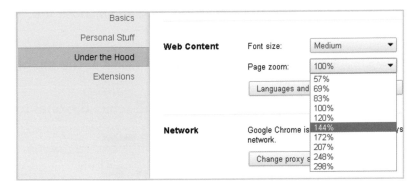

- In Safari, click the Settings icon and click Preferences. To change the appearance, use the Appearance tab.

 HOT TIP: Once you find the configuration options for your web browser, explore every tab and option so you're aware of what's available.

 DID YOU KNOW?
Internet Explorer also offers a Settings icon where you can access Internet Options.

 HOT TIP: If you can't see the Tools menu, tap the Alt key.

 HOT TIP: If you change the default font size, zoom size or other font settings, web pages may not look exactly as you'd expect.

Show toolbars and menus

If you use the File, Edit or View menus often and are tired of tapping the Alt key to access them, you can make the Menu bar available all the time. If you want your favourite bookmarks and favourites to be available, you show those too. There are often several toolbars to choose from.

- To show toolbars in Internet Explorer or Firefox, right click at the top of the window and select the toolbars to show.
- To show toolbars in Safari, click the Settings icon and select the ones to show.

- To show toolbars in Chrome, click the wrench icon. Then, click Bookmarks to show the Bookmarks bar.

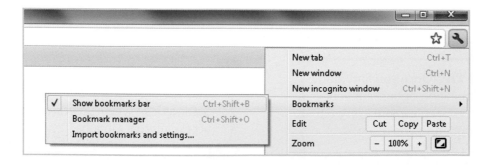

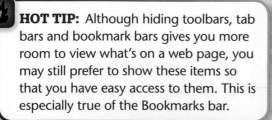 **HOT TIP:** Although hiding toolbars, tab bars and bookmark bars gives you more room to view what's on a web page, you may still prefer to show these items so that you have easy access to them. This is especially true of the Bookmarks bar.

Use thumbnail views

Most browsers offer a way to view thumbnails of the sites you visit most, so that you can easily access those sites later, even without bookmarking them. For instance, in Internet Explorer, from a new, blank tab, you can click any thumbnail to access a site that you visit often.

- Firefox offers a Most Visited option from the Bookmarks toolbar.
- In Chrome you can click the wrench icon and click History, or sign in with a Google account and create additional customisations.
- In Safari, click the Show Top Sites icon from the Bookmarks bar. This also has to be enabled in Settings>Preferences>Bookmarks.

HOT TIP: A book this size could be filled with information about how to use the four browsers introduced in this chapter. What's offered here is just a small sample of what you can do.

HOT TIP: All web browsers offer a Help option, a home page and forums to share ideas and ask questions. Visit these areas to learn more about any browser.

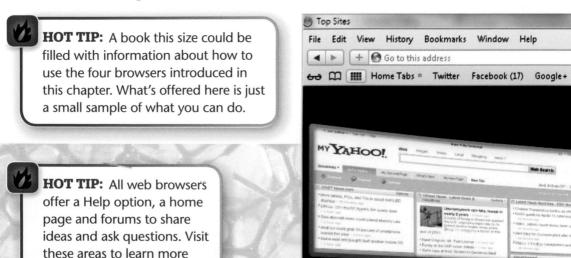

Be mindful of the Address bar

Every web browser has an Address bar, even if it is called something else (perhaps a 'location' bar). This bar tells you quite a bit about the website you're visiting. You should be mindful of the Address bar, especially after leaving a site you trust for one you're not sure of.

- Make sure the website you're visiting is the one you want to visit. www.bbc.com is not even close to what you'll see if you visit www.bbc.org or www.bbbc.com.

- If you see https://, you're browsing a secure site. It's okay to make purchases here and input personal information.

- If you do not see https:// but instead see something else, do not make purchases from the website or input personally identifiable information like your credit card information.

- http:// implies the site is a website you can browse, and most websites start with this prefix.

- Any time you visit a financial website, make sure your bank name is listed just after https://www. If it is something else, close the browser immediately and try again.

- If you see something other than http or https, you are into new territory and should carefully consider what you're doing. In the case of FTP, you'll be sharing files.

ftp://ftp.pearsoned-ema.com/

? DID YOU KNOW?

When you click a link in a phishing email, instead of being taken to, say, www.chase.com you may instead be taken to something like www.mychaseweb3358x.com. Always make sure by checking the Address bar.

! ALERT: File sharing websites such as those that start with FTP can be dangerous and should be avoided. Exceptions are in order if you've been instructed by say, a publisher, to use that site to swap files.

Avoid installing toolbars and add-ons

A web browser, as time passes, will often take longer to start, require more time to produce search results, load pages slowly or even stop responding completely. There are many reasons for this, but most of the time it's because of the additional add-ons, extensions and toolbars you've opted to install. You should occasionally review and disable unwanted add-ons and extensions for optimal performance.

- In Internet Explorer, click Tools and Manage add-ons. From there you can disable unwanted items easily.

- In Firefox, click Tools and Add-ons. Explore Extensions and Plugins to see what you've attached.

- In Safari, click the Settings icon and then Preferences. Explore the Extensions tab to see what's running.

- In Chrome, click the wrench icon, Tools, and then Extensions to see what's running.

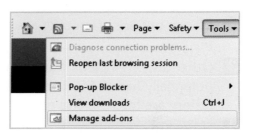

ALERT: If you disable add-ons that you need, you'll probably be prompted to enable them when they are required.

HOT TIP: You can delete cookies in all browsers. Cookies contain information about your web preferences when you visit a site. They are what allow you to be greeted with Hello, followed by your name, at Amazon. com, for instance. Deleting cookies probably won't make a noticeable performance difference though, and if you do delete cookies you'll have to re-enter your user name and password for *all* of the sites you visit.

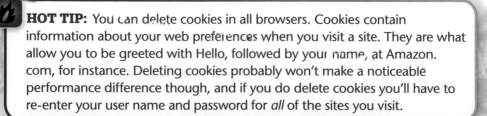

Explore safety and security options

All web browsers offer safety and security options. What's available and how to configure the options differ from browser to browser, but all have similar characteristics and purposes.

1 The security options generally offer a way to define the level of security you need. The default setting is generally appropriate.

2 Privacy options often offer a way to stop websites from tracking your movements on the web.

3 Other options include the ability to stop pop-up advertisements, warn you of potentially harmful websites, start a private browsing session where no cookies or history are tracked, and more.

4 Some browsers even offer parental controls (or grand-parental controls!).

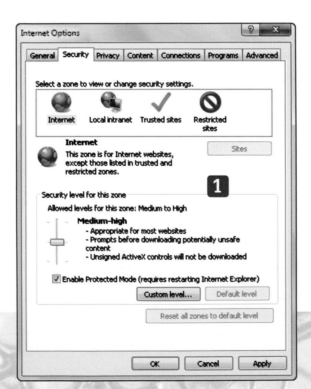

6 Avoiding phishing, pop-ups, ads and other website threats

Introduction

You have probably learned that postal mail you receive touting the best weight loss drug ever or the newest miracle cure for ageing is a scam. You've learned not to trust what you see in junk faxes too. Of course, you learned a long time ago not to give any information to telephone salespeople, not even your name.

Your first line of defence against falling for web scams is to be just as sceptical, because you will encounter threats while surfing the internet. They may be in the form of unassuming advertisements or obvious phishing attacks from websites, or the threat could come from someone you know that has access to your web browsing history from your own personal computer. A threat could be looming in the background, through a security hole that can only be rectified by installing a web browser update. Of course, you could fall into a trap by visiting the wrong type of website too, which is why you must remain sceptical and cautious about the websites you intentionally visit.

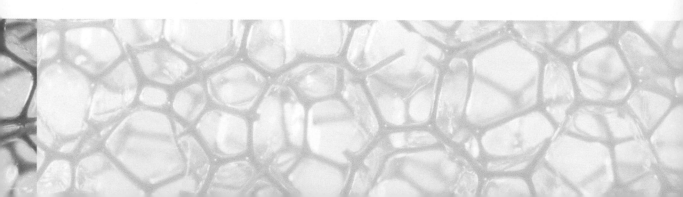

Don't click ads!

Advertisements can be dangerous. Clicking a pop-up advertisement could invoke a worm or virus. Clicking an advertisement on a web page could take you to a site that is unsafe, is a phishing website, or one that is laden with viruses, adware, malware and other threats. You'll find advertisements in various places, and it's important to avoid all of them.

1. When you search for something from a website such as Google, Yahoo!, Bing and others, often the first few search results listed are paid ads. Scroll down until you get to the real results.

2. Ads appear on the right side of search results too, as well as on web pages you personalise.

3. Ads can appear in pop-up windows. Never click these ads, only click the X to close them.

4. Ads appear on social networking sites often in the right-hand column.

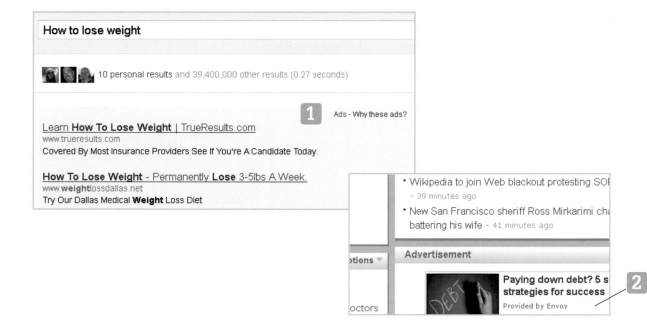

Enable a pop-up blocker

All of the popular web browsers come with a pop-up blocker that is enabled by default. You should check to make sure though, just to be safe. You access the pop-up blocker settings the same way you accessed configuration, personalisation, safety and/or security settings in Chapter 5. Here's how to access the settings in Internet Explorer and Firefox.

1 In Internet Explorer:

   a Click Tools.

   b Click Pop-up Blocker.

   c Verify the pop-up blocker is enabled.

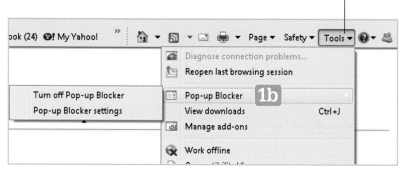

2 In Firefox:

   a Click Tools then Options.

   b Click the Content tab.

   c Verify that Block pop-up windows is enabled.

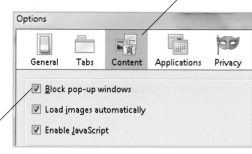

? DID YOU KNOW?

Other web browsers allow you to verify that pop-ups are blocked too. If you can't find the setting, search the web for 'block pop-ups in' followed by the name of your web browser.

? DID YOU KNOW?

Sometimes you need to allow a pop-up for a site. If this is the case, hold down the Alt key when clicking the link that produces a pop-up.

Skip ads that appear on web pages

Sometimes when you visit a web page, perhaps to get information about a product or to gain access to data on it, an ad will appear. Often the ad will play for 30 seconds or so before it goes away on its own. The option to close the ad before it runs its course is often unavailable or hidden. Here are some places to look for the option to skip the ad.

- Look at the top right corner of the ad for a small x. You may have to move your mouse there for it to appear.
- Look for the option to Skip, Skip this Ad, or Collapse.
- If you accidentally click an ad, know that you'll be taken to a website for the product, and away from the site you're trying to access. Click the Back button as soon as you can.
- Look for an option to Enter Site.

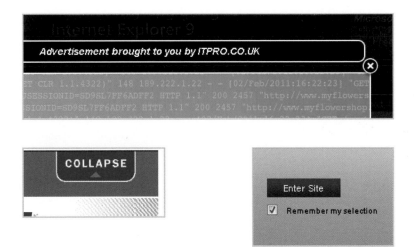

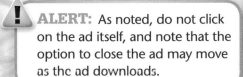

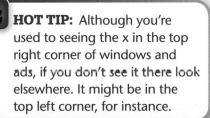

ALERT: As noted, do not click on the ad itself, and note that the option to close the ad may move as the ad downloads.

HOT TIP: Although you're used to seeing the x in the top right corner of windows and ads, if you don't see it there look elsewhere. It might be in the top left corner, for instance.

Avoid phishing websites

A phishing website is one that tries to trick you into revealing personal information, such as your name, address, date of birth, user names and passwords to websites, and even your credit card or mortgage information. With many web browsers, you'll be prompted when you visit a site that's been previously reported. You should verify that any related phishing features are enabled, and take heed when you are warned.

- In Internet Explorer, enable the SmartScreen Filter. It's located under the Safety option.

- In Firefox, click Tools then Options, and verify the security features here are enabled.

- In Safari, click the Settings icon, Preferences, and then the Security tab. Verify the Fraudulent Sites option is enabled.

- In Chrome, click the wrench, Options, and then Under the Hood. Select Enable phishing and malware protection.

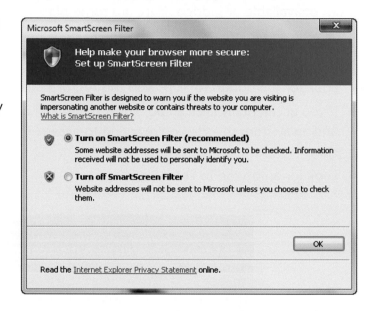

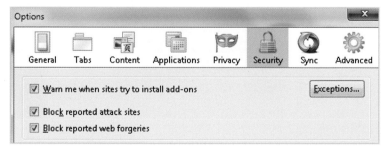

ALERT: If you see a notice that the website you are visiting is a possible phishing or fraudulent website, click the Back button or close the browser immediately.

? DID YOU KNOW?
In Internet Explorer 9 you can check a website for threats from Safety, SmartScreen Filter, and Check this website.

Report an unsafe website

Browsers often offer a place to report an unsafe website. The option, if available, usually appears with the phishing options outlined in the previous section. As an example, here's how to report an unsafe website using Internet Explorer 9. Do this only if you are at the website you believe is fraudulent or a threat.

1 Click Safety.

2 Click SmartScreen Filter.

3 Click Report unsafe website.

? DID YOU KNOW?

In Firefox you can click Tools and then Page Info to learn more about the web page you're visiting, including how many times you've visited it in the past. You can assume if you've visited the page often, it's the actual site where you pay your bill, do your banking or access other data.

🔥 HOT TIP: If you visit a website that is fraudulent and mimicking a real site (perhaps your bank or mortgage company), report the site to the institution being mimicked. Do this even if you can locate the option to report the site via your web browser.

? DID YOU KNOW?

In Firefox, click Help and Report Web Forgery to report a fraudulent website.

Understand cookies

Cookies are small text files that websites place on your computer. Each file only relates to a single website. The text files contain information about your name, preferences, your user name and your password, among other things. Cookies are generally harmless. However, there is an option to delete all cookies and to never accept cookies from websites, just in case you'd like to.

1 Open the Settings or Preferences options for your web browser.

2 Locate the Privacy or Security options.

3 Locate the option to delete cookies or configure them.

4 Consider keeping the defaults to block cookies from third parties and advertisers.

5 Consider if it's an option, to accept cookies from 'first parties' and block those from 'third parties'.

? DID YOU KNOW?

If you disable cookies from *all* websites, many sites won't work as expected. Cookies are often a requirement.

! ALERT: If you delete the cookies for websites you've visited, you'll have to reenter your user names and passwords when you visit those sites again.

? DID YOU KNOW?

If you have a problem with your web browser that you can't fix, you may be prompted by a help file or a help forum to delete the cookies on your machine. This rarely helps, but you should do it if nothing else works.

Delete browsing history

All web browsers keep track of the websites you've visited. How long that data is kept depends on the browser, but it is often around three weeks. If you share a computer with someone and you don't want them to see the websites you've recently visited, you can delete your browsing history.

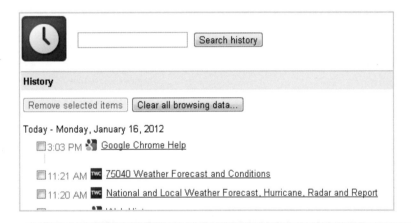

- In Internet Explorer, click Safety, then Delete browsing history.
- In Firefox, click Tools, and then Clear recent history.
- In Chrome, click the wrench, click History, click Edit items, and click Clear all browsing data.
- In Safari, from the Menu bar, click History, and then click Clear history.

DID YOU KNOW?

Grandchildren often know how to access the browsing history on a computer, and can figure out where you've been shopping and what you may have bought them for their birthday or Christmas!

HOT TIP: To show the Menu bar in Safari, Internet Explorer or Firefox, tap the Alt key on the keyboard.

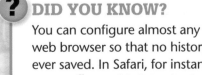

DID YOU KNOW?

You can configure almost any web browser so that no history is ever saved. In Safari, for instance, you configure this from Settings, Preferences, and the General tab.

Keep your browsers up to date

The companies that create web browsers often offer updates that have new features, new functionality, and yes, fix security flaws. It's important to install these updates when they become available. How those updates become available depends on many factors including what operating system is installed on your computer and what web browser you're using.

- If you use a Windows-based computer, make sure that Windows Update is enabled and set to install updates automatically.

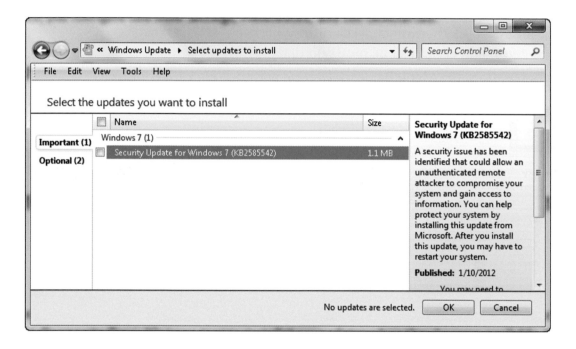

- If you use an Apple computer, set updates to install automatically, and opt to install any when prompted.

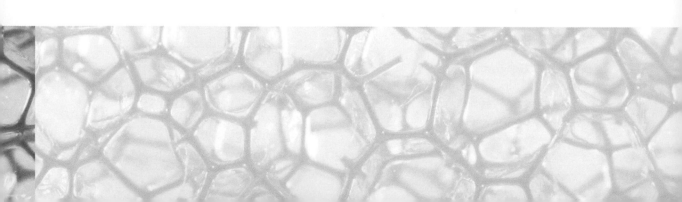

- No matter what web browser you use, make sure it's set to get updates automatically. Below the setting for Firefox is shown.

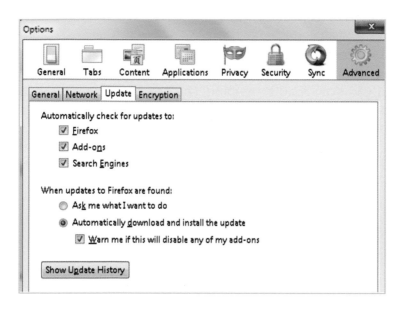

- Sometimes companies create entirely new web browsers that are seemingly more than a simple update. Here is an option to try out IE10.

Experience IE10
Download Now!

? DID YOU KNOW?
Some updates that are meant for your computer will often fix security issues associated with the internet too.

🔥 HOT TIP: Unless you're a geek, avoid beta and test versions of upcoming web browsers. They may be bug infested or have missing features.

Consider private browsing options

All of the major web browsers offer an option to surf the internet privately, without collecting cookies, naming the sites you visit in your History list, or saving user names and passwords. If you download something, the download won't appear after the fact in any download lists either. How you go about starting a private browsing session depends on the web browser you're using.

- In Internet Explorer, click the New Tab icon to the right of existing, open tabs. Click In Private Browsing.
- In Firefox, from the Menu bar click Tools, and then click Start Private Browsing.
- In Safari, click the Settings icon and click Private Browsing.
- In Chrome, click the wrench and click New incognito window.

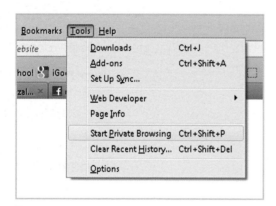
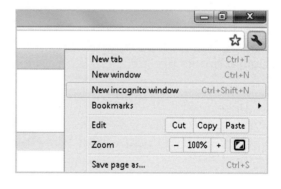

7 Shopping safely on the web

Introduction

Buying products from the internet is convenient and often the best way to make purchases, provided you do so safely. You can buy unique gifts from around the world; books, music and videos from places like the Amazon Kindle Store and Apple's iTunes store; necessities from your favourite local companies; and clothing from department stores. You can even buy food from grocery chains. You can buy both new and used items at auctions too, like those offered on eBay. You can purchase and activate a mobile phone, electricity service and more, all without leaving your house.

While buying from the internet may be a convenience, it can be necessity too. Perhaps you no longer want to drive or feel safe on public transport, or health problems have left you without the stamina to shop. Perhaps you live in a secluded area. Maybe you need to buy a gift and mail it, but don't have a post office nearby and can't travel to one. Whatever the case, you need to know who you can trust online, where you can shop, and how to shop safely. You'll learn all of that here!

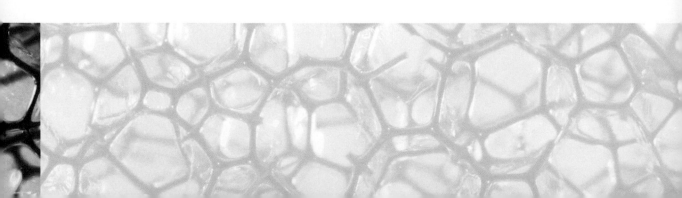

Find websites you can trust

In this day and age it's hard to know who you can trust. However, if you stay with companies you've done business with before and those your friends and family suggest, you can be sure you'll have a good, safe, buying experience. Here are some considerations for making safe purchases online.

- Only buy from companies you already know and trust, and have had successful transactions with in the past.
- Make major purchases from well-known entities like Amazon, Apple, Microsoft and the like.
- Make purchases from department stores you already shop from and perhaps even have credit cards with.
- For now, avoid places like eBay until you've learned more about staying safe on the internet.
- Avoid making purchases from overseas locations.
- Only make purchases from websites that start with https://.

ALERT: If you are purchasing software, read the reviews first. Read reviews of the company that is selling the software too.

? DID YOU KNOW?
You can create an ongoing order at many websites so that items you use often will be delivered on a schedule. For instance, you can have Amazon send you shampoo and conditioner once every two months, automatically.

! ALERT: Making purchases from overseas sellers is discouraged because not only will it be hard to return the item if you don't like it, it will be nearly impossible to get your money back if you get scammed.

Look for third-party seals of approval

There are third-parties whose business it is to give seals of approval to products. You may already be familiar with Trusted Shops or the Better Business Bureau. A good review from CNet can be considered a seal of approval for tech products as well. When buying online look for seals of approval from entities you trust.

1 Visit a website you trust or have purchased from before.

2 Look for any seals of approval from entities you know.

3 Look for the product you wish to buy.

4 See if those products are on any trusted third-party seal of approval lists.

? DID YOU KNOW?

Not all companies are certified by the Better Business Bureau. That doesn't mean they aren't good, legitimate and trusted businesses though.

Read reviews

Just about all websites that sell products offer customer reviews. Some offer them from all buyers in a listing below the product information. Some offer selected reviews from selected customers as 'testimonials' on a web page. The latter may be biased though, so you have to be careful there.

1 From any website that sells products, navigate to the product you'd like to buy.

2 Click the link to access the customer reviews.

3 Read the reviews, noting that often you can sort the reviews by their ratings or authors.

Windows 7 in Simple Steps [Paperback]
Joli Ballew ☑ (Author)
★★★★☆ ☑ (5 customer reviews) 👍 Like (0)

2

RRP: £10.99
Price: **£7.69** & this item **Delivered FREE in the UK** with Sup
You Save: £3.30 (30%)

In stock.
Dispatched from and sold by **Amazon.co.uk**. Gift-wrap available.

Customer Reviews
Windows 7 in Simple Steps

5 Reviews

5 star:	(4)
4 star:	(0)
3 star:	(1)
2 star:	(0)
1 star:	(0)

Average Customer Review
★★★★☆ (5 customer reviews)

Share your thoughts with other customers

[Create your own review]

The most helpful favourable review

2 of 2 people found the following review helpful:

3

★★★★★ **Book Review**
Excellent book, simple to read. Found it very useful learning abou
system. Wish all books were this good.
Published 16 months ago by Mr. M. F. Irwin

› See more **5 star**, 4 star reviews

HOT TIP: Not all bad reviews are a reflection of the product; after reading the reviews you may find that a poor review didn't have much to do with the product at all. It may be that the product took too long to arrive, was damaged on arrival, or was not the right size or colour and was difficult to return.

WHAT DOES THIS MEAN?

Testimonial: this is a good review written by someone who has used the product or was paid to use it. Sometimes, those that write testimonials are also paid for their positive review!

Create strong passwords

To buy a product from Amazon and other places, you have to have a user name and password, and you have to provide an email address for order confirmations. Although creating strong passwords was covered in Chapter 1, it bears repeating here.

- Create passwords that are at least six characters long. The longer the better.
- Include upper and lower case letters.
- Include at least one number.
- Include one or more special symbols.
- Create passwords that you can remember with a little effort, like MyAccountIsAtAmaz0nUK74.

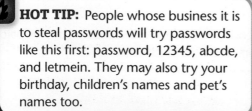 **HOT TIP:** People whose business it is to steal passwords will try passwords like this first: password, 12345, abcde, and letmein. They may also try your birthday, children's names and pet's names too.

 **DID YOU KNOW?**
To protect your account at online shopping websites, log out when you are finished shopping at the site.

8 Using social networking sites safely

Introduction

The most popular social networking site in the world is Facebook. Twitter comes in second in popularity, LinkedIn third, and MySpace and Google+ follow those. There are some up-and-comers though, including MyLife and MeetUp, among others. If you use these sites, you should know how to use them safely.

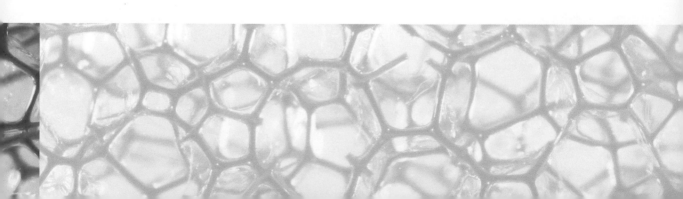

Know which social networks to use

Although this chapter is about staying safe while using social networking websites, it's important to understand the purpose of each site you use and try to use each one accordingly.

- Facebook – most people use this site to share details about their lives, and want to communicate with family, friends, acquaintances, childhood friends, coworkers and former classmates.

- Twitter – people use this site to write short messages to anyone who cares to read them, often for the purpose of promoting themselves, their business or their interests.

HOT TIP: If you're just getting into social networking, create an account with and use Facebook for your personal updates. Then, create an account with and use LinkedIn for your professional ones.

? DID YOU KNOW?
The social networking sites here are all free, although LinkedIn does offer an upgraded account type you can opt to pay for.

- LinkedIn – people use this site to share their professional persona. You'll use LinkedIn to connect to potential employers and clients, to find jobs, to network with other professionals, and so on.

- MySpace – it seems that the major clientele for MySpace is budding musicians, teenagers and tweens, although there are more people than that using it. You might find your grandson's garage band here.
- Google+ – this up and coming social networking site is gaining ground, is similar to Facebook, but lets you group friends into circles and communicate with them in various ways.

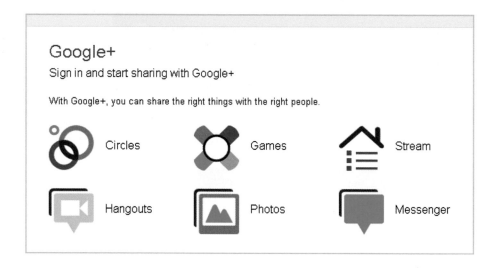

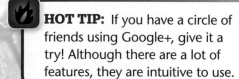

DID YOU KNOW?

Twitter is mainly used to disseminate information quickly, such as breaking news, the length of the queue at a favourite restaurant or the latest celebrity break-up.

HOT TIP: If you have a circle of friends using Google+, give it a try! Although there are a lot of features, they are intuitive to use.

Protect your password

No matter what password you create, strong or weak, long or short, you must protect it. If someone finds out your user name and password for a website, they can cause a lot of problems. Imagine what a disgruntled employee or angry grandchild could post on Facebook or LinkedIn, pretending to be you! The results could be devastating. Here are a few ideas for protecting your password.

- Commit your password to memory and tear up any notes you've written regarding it.
- If you can't commit your password to memory, write it down and keep it in a locked box or safe.
- Don't leave your password in plain sight or where someone might look for it, like in a desk drawer or the underside of your keyboard tray.
- If you must keep your password written down and handy, consider writing down only a portion of it or a cryptic version.
- Opt to hide password characters on websites if applicable.
- If you share a computer with others, opt not to let websites remember your password or keep you logged in.

 HOT TIP: If your password is MyDogHasFleaz75, write it down as ##MyDogHasFleaz$$75##. Only you will know to take out the special characters when entering it.

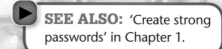 **SEE ALSO:** 'Create strong passwords' in Chapter 1.

Learn what you should never share online

One of the first things to know about staying safe when using social websites is what not to share with others. Here are a few things you should never share anywhere, including Facebook, Twitter, LinkedIn and similar websites.

- Your physical address or phone number.
- Credit card, banking or financial information.
- When you'll be away on holiday and for how long (if you must post, always state you have a house sitter).
- When you're leaving your home unattended.
- The full names, ages, addresses and so on, of your children, friends or relatives.
- Pictures of new, expensive purchases.
- How much you dislike your boss or coworkers.

Know what you're sharing by default

When you sign up to be a member of a social network, you input some degree of information about yourself. You may put your date of birth, where you work, your interests and your political views, to name a few. You need to know how much of that is being shared with others. Here's how to find out on Facebook (other websites are similar).

1 To see what you've added to Facebook, click your name in the top right corner.

2 Scroll down to see what's shown.

3 The items you see that do not have a lock by them are available for others to see.

4 Click the down arrow to quickly 'unshare' personal information.

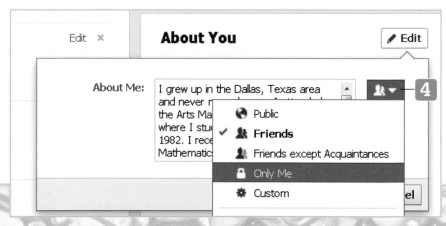

? DID YOU KNOW?
Items with a lock beside them aren't shared with others.

! ALERT: It's probably best to hide most of the information you're currently sharing. People don't need to know your birthdate, where you went to primary school and so on.

Limit who can view your profile

You can limit who can view your profile. Some social networking sites offer more options for limiting your profile than others, though. For instance, on Twitter, by default your profile is public, and what you input is available to anyone who wants to see it.

- On Twitter, you can protect all tweets by selecting Protect My Tweets in Account Settings.
- On LinkedIn, click your name and then Settings to change how information is shared.
- On Facebook, myriad settings are available from Privacy Settings.

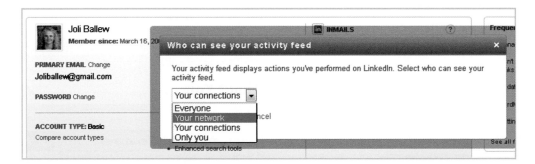

? DID YOU KNOW?

Sometimes it's difficult to locate the exact setting you're looking for to keep a specific bit of information private. An easier way to hide what's available is to delete it from your profile altogether, as detailed in the next section.

? DID YOU KNOW?

Twitter offers accounts that are protected, where only followers you approve of can view your tweets (posts). No one can *retweet* what you've written either.

2 To unsubscribe from someone on Facebook:

a Wait for an offending post to appear.

b Click the right arrow beside the post.

c Click the desired option, probably Unsubscribe.

d Note that you can opt to unsubscribe only from a specific thing they post, like a game or photos.

Unhighlight this story
Hide story
Report story or spam

Subscribed to Karen
✓ **All Updates**
Most Updates
Only Important

Unsubscribe from Karen
Unsubscribe from photos by Karen — 2d

3 To completely block a person on Facebook:

a Navigate to their page.

b Click the Settings icon.

c Click Report/Block.

d Choose the desired setting (unsubscribe, unfriend, block).

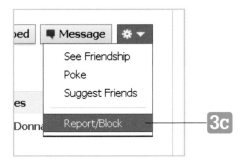

See Friendship
Poke
Suggest Friends

Report/Block — 3c

? DID YOU KNOW?

When you block a person's game status updates, you block updates for that game from everyone in your network.

! ALERT: Completely blocking someone should be used as a last resort, because the person will know you've blocked them and there may be a confrontation. They will not know you've unsubscribed or hidden all of their posts though, which makes these much less drastic options.

Learn how to ask someone to remove content

Having a bit too much to drink and living to regret it the day after (in the privacy of your own home) is nothing compared to waking up to photos of yourself dancing on a table wearing virtually nothing, on someone else's Facebook, Twitter, Google+ or MySpace page. It happens. If you find undesirable content on the internet, you can probably ask the owner to remove it. This example uses Facebook.

1 Locate the inappropriate content.

2 Locate the owner's name.

3 Contact the person (via private message) and ask them to remove the item.

4 If they do not remove the item, return to the page and select the option to report it.

| vis | Album: | Photos |
| uary 16 | Shared with: ✸ Custom | |

🏷 Tag This Photo
📍 Add Location

Download
Report This Photo 4

? DID YOU KNOW?
You can remove your own posts by clicking the arrow to the right of it and clicking Edit/Remove.

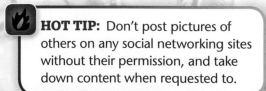

HOT TIP: Don't post pictures of others on any social networking sites without their permission, and take down content when requested to.

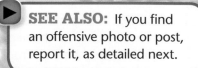

SEE ALSO: If you find an offensive photo or post, report it, as detailed next.

Report abusive content

Some content is downright disgusting. Often you can report such content to the website. It may or may not be taken down, but you'll feel better about it anyway. You may also need to report a photo of you that someone took and then posted without your permission.

Because so many millions of people use Facebook, the remaining sections in this chapter will deal with Facebook exclusively.

1 Locate the offensive material.

2 Click the option to report it.

3 Select the desired options and click Continue.

Is this photo about you or a friend?

Yes, this photo is about me or a friend:
- ○ I don't like this photo of me
- ○ It's harassing me
- ○ It's harassing a friend

No, this photo is about something else:
- ○ Spam or scam
- ● Nudity or pornography
- ○ Graphic violence
- ○ Hate speech or symbol
- ○ Illegal drug use

Is this your intellectual property?   **Continue**   **Cancel**

? DID YOU KNOW?

It's better to write to a person directly through a message if the picture is of you and you'd like it removed. It's best to report to Facebook if it's pornography or something equally vile.

4 Choose how to report the content. Click Continue.

5 Complete the process as required.

4

What You Can Do

Learn about the Facebook Community Standards.

○ **Message** **to remove**
   Ask to remove the photo
○ **Block**
   You and will no longer be able to see each other or connect on Facebook

☐ Report to Facebook   **Continue** **Cancel**

4

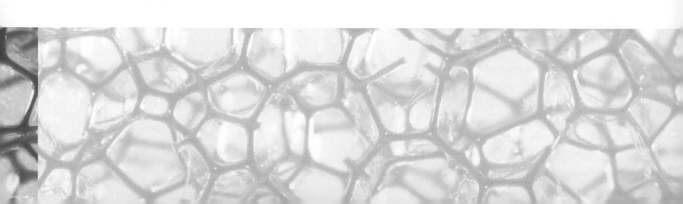

Be careful what you click

There are a lot of games available to play on Facebook. There are lots of apps too, as well as videos to view, pictures to see and links to click. The same is true on other social networking sites. Unfortunately, some of these items will contain adware or other malware that can infect your computer, compromise your account and more. It's hard, at least at first, to know what's okay to click and what isn't.

- If you want to watch a video, visit www.snopes.com and type the name of the video in the Search window. Make sure it's not a virus or a scam.
- If you want to play a game, ask your friends if they've played it first.
- If you're unsure of a game, use Google.com to search and see if the game is safe to play.
- To learn more about staying safe, visit the website's Security pages.

15 Seconds

Virus: "Nobody can watch this for more than 15 seconds" video.

....

● **REAL SCAM**

....

How To Play Safe & Avoid FarmVille Scams

How-To Topics » scams, Farmville, farmville cash, farm ville, facebook scams, farmville scams, cash scams, game scams,

! ALERT: Until you know more about using social network sites, avoid installing apps, viewing 'must-see' videos and agreeing to let an app access your account.

▶ SEE ALSO: 'Be careful with Facebook games', next.

Be careful with Facebook games

People get addicted to Facebook games. It's true, and you could be next! Before you start down this road, research what the game is about, and really consider how you want to spend your time! If you do decide to get involved in a game like FarmVille or CityVille, consider the following.

- You'll have to give the game specific permission to access various parts of your account.
- You'll have to post repeatedly to obtain items for the game, which will probably annoy your friends.
- You may have to make purchases to move forward in a game. These can add up.
- You may get addicted.

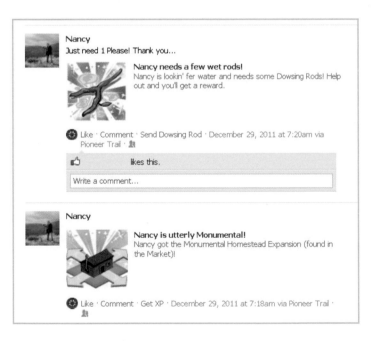

 ALERT: Research the game using Google or Bing before starting to play. Make sure you understand how the game is played and what will be required of you (money, permissions, getting others to play, etc.)

HOT TIP: If you do decide to play a game that requires you post often, inform your network you're doing so. Tell networkers they can easily unsubscribe from games updates while still remaining subscribed and friends with you.

Learn how to protect your social networking account

You already know how to create a strong password, and you know not to keep it taped to the underside of your keyboard. Here are a few other options for protecting your social networking account.

- Avoid giving any app permission to access your account.
- Change your password every two or three months.
- Don't give your password to your fiancé, spouse, children or grandchildren.
- Log out of the computer or out of all social network sites so others can't access it while you're away from the computer.
- Don't let a website remember your password; type it in each time.
- If options exist to always connect securely, select them.
- If you know you're not going to use an account, deactivate it.

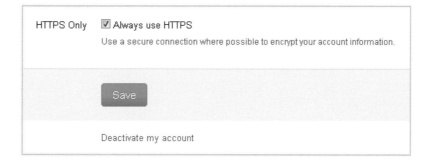

HTTPS Only   ☑ Always use HTTPS
Use a secure connection where possible to encrypt your account information.

[Save]

Deactivate my account

 HOT TIP: If someone figures out your password, change it right away.

 HOT TIP: Make sure people can't see you type your password.

9 Sharing your personal information on the web

Introduction

You may be surprised at just how much information is available about you on the internet. If you 'Google' yourself, you may find your physical address and a picture of your house, photos and videos of you and your family, and where you went to high school or college. Although there's not much you can do now about what's already on the internet without some serious legwork, you can prevent more information from becoming available in the future.

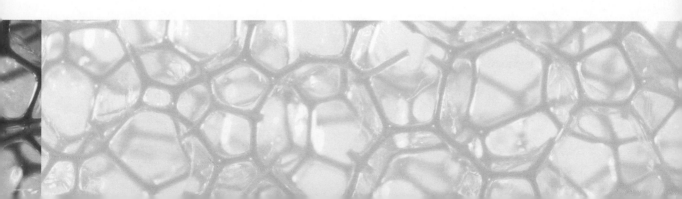

Register only if it's mandatory

You are constantly asked to register at websites and to register products you buy. The registration process may ask for your name, address, phone number, age, date of birth and even your total income, among other things. When registration is mandatory and the questions are invasive though, you can still register, but understand that you don't always have to tell the truth!

- Register with accurate information at financial institutions.
- If a website only asks you to create a screen name, provide an email address, and create a password, go ahead and register if you want to use the site. Make sure to opt out of additional correspondence, though.
- A general website should not need to know your physical address to allow you to post your thoughts or reply to others.
- 99% of websites should never need to know your age or date of birth.
- A website should certainly never ask for your household income. If it does, opt not to answer, lie or simply choose not to register.

Sign up through CNN only:

Screen name

This can't be changed later!
Use 3-12 characters; Numbers and letters only

E-mail

Make sure you typed it correctly.
You will receive an e-mail to validate your account

Password

Make it 6-10 characters, no spaces

Type what you see in the grey box

XC8247

If you can't read this, try another one.

 HOT TIP: If you have to register at a website to gain access to features of it (to personalise it or to post to it), you don't have to give your real age, your real address, etc. Most websites don't need this information.

 HOT TIP: If you are asked to register when filling out a warranty form, just give your name and address, and the required product numbers. If you have to use the warranty later, they can find you with that information alone.

? DID YOU KNOW?
Some websites you register with should be configured with actual, real information, including banks, mortgage companies, credit card companies and the like.

Create screen names carefully

When you're sure you are ready to register for a website, think of the name you'd like others to see when you post your thoughts, upload photos or videos, or make comments. If you use your real name, understand that you're revealing your true identity to strangers. This may not be a big deal if your name is John Smith, but if your name is Joli Ballew, well, that's a different story.

- Create a screen name that is easy to remember and read.
- Understand that others who view any content you've uploaded or typed will see your screen name.
- Be creative!
- If registration fails, look for the reason why. You should see a prompt.
- Once you've created a screen name, write down the screen name and password for reference later.

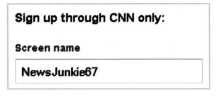

That screen name is already taken. Please choose another.

HOT TIP: If you register for and post often to similar websites, consider using the same screen name if you can. It will help identify you to others who enjoy your material.

? DID YOU KNOW?

The screen name you want may already be taken. Websites don't allow you to use a screen name that someone else is already using.

Know how to post anonymously

If you want to post something to a website, newsgroup or forum, or even to YouTube, you'll have to register and sign in. Most of the time, you can't post anonymously, although occasionally you will see the option to post as a guest. However, you can create a user name that does not identify you in any way.

1 When prompted to sign in, consider creating a new account just for that website.

2 Click Sign In, Sign Up, or Register.

3 If you want to participate in the forums anonymously, create a new user ID that is not already associated with the website.

ALERT: When creating an ID that is to be associated with an account you can make purchases with, such as an Apple ID or one at Amazon, you will be prompted for your birthdate and primary address, among other things. You may even be prompted to input credit card information. You'll have to decide if you really want to do this.

WHAT DOES THIS MEAN?

Newsgroups and **forums**: these are often places where users ask questions and other users answer them. Apple calls it a **community**. A **post** is what you type.

Share photos safely

You learned in Chapter 8 that you can share photos on social networking sites like Facebook and limit who sees those photos through your account and privacy settings. You can control who sees photos on other photo websites too, including Flickr and Picasa. There's more to it when it comes to posting photos safely, though; here are some additional tips.

- Never post inappropriate content; you never know when someone in your family may decide to run for public office.
- Know that when you 'tag' photos, you're revealing your identity to others.
- Disable GPS technology before taking a photo with your smartphone and posting it.
- Don't post photos that could embarrass your children or grandchildren.

Learn how to blog safely

A blog is an online journal. It may be a diary of personal events, a place to vent frustrations or a way to promote yourself. It's very easy to offer too much personal information in a blog, including where you live, where you work out, where you shop, and so on. If you're going to blog, be careful!

- Before you start a blog, research how to blog safely.
- Choose a reputable blog website like WordPress.
- Keep in mind your readers may include your boss, children or neighbours.
- If you're going to blog about, say, your workout regimen, avoid naming your gym.
- If you're going to blog about your frustrations or your job, create a screen name no one will recognise.
- Continually ask yourself how easy it would be to find you, should someone want to.

ALERT: There have been reports of blog 'stalkers'. It's scary. If you ever feel threatened, tell the police, the blog site and anyone else who will listen. You may also want to disable your blog for a while until the stalker loses interest.

Be careful what you share on dating websites

There are a handful of reputable senior dating websites (if you're a senior), but you still have to be safe. Here are some tips for creating your online dating profile and communicating with strangers:

- Choose a dating website that is recognised and well known.
- Follow any advice regarding how to create your profile.
- Don't put anything in your online profile you would not tell a stranger.
- Before you hand over your address and phone number, get to know your potential match via email or chat rooms, text chats and video chats, in that order.
- Type your potential date's name into a Google search window with quotes around it. Add any other information such as city name or birthday to find out more.

A Guide to Writing your online Profile

We want everyone's profiles to be as good as possible so that all our Members stand a better chance of finding what they're looking for on the site so we thought it would be a good idea to give everyone a few pointers as to **what makes a good profile.**

! ALERT: Take things slowly, and avoid meeting a potential date in person until you've had time to fully check out their profile and history.

? DID YOU KNOW? There are companies available who will, for a nominal fee, run a background check on potential dates.

Be careful what you post on YouTube

You should incorporate all you've learned so far when posting to YouTube. You'll need to be careful when creating a screen name, avoid posting material you may regret later, and be mindful that others may not want to be on YouTube! Of course, don't share your address or phone number, or share any credit card information.

1 Create an account on YouTube.com.

2 Log in with that account.

3 Click Upload.

4 Click Select Files from Your Computer.

5 Select the file and click Open.

6 While the video uploads, type a title and a description.

3

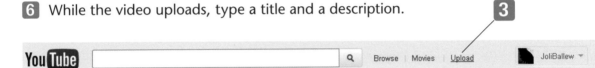

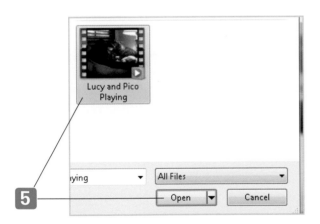

5

> 🔥 **HOT TIP:** You may want to show your real name on YouTube if you are using the website for self promotion.

> ❓ **DID YOU KNOW?**
> You'll need to register and log in to post video to YouTube.

> ❓ **DID YOU KNOW?**
> YouTube offers privacy options. Click the arrow by your user name, click Settings, and then click Privacy.

Explore ways to expunge information from the web

Once something is on the internet, unless it belongs to you, such as a photo or video you've posted on YouTube, Picasa, Facebook and the like, it's difficult to get it removed. If you find something threatening, or something that directly affects you or your privacy, there are sometimes actions you can take. At the website where the material resides, try the following.

1 Make a note of who posted the material, and contact them to remove it. If they don't, continue here.

2 Locate the safety, privacy or security center.

3 Click any option that enables you to file a complaint or request material be removed.

4 Work through the process required to notify the website of the type of problem you're having.

5 Complete any complaint processes, and wait for a response from the website.

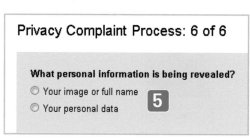

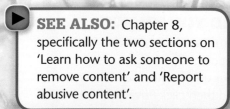

SEE ALSO: Chapter 8, specifically the two sections on 'Learn how to ask someone to remove content' and 'Report abusive content'.

Look for your house on Google Maps

To end this chapter, let's take a look at some additional information on the internet that may unnerve you. To get started, use any web browser to navigate to www.maps.google.co.uk.

1 At maps.google.co.uk, type your address or the address of some place you visit often.

2 Double-click the icon that appears there. If you don't see an icon, click in an area nearby or type a different address.

3 Take a look at the picture that appears. Drag to see different views.

? **DID YOU KNOW?**
You won't see photos of every place in the UK, but you will see photos of many, including your own home.

? **DID YOU KNOW?**
The pictures you see of places you locate using Google Maps were taken some time ago. Faces and licence plates are blurred out.

🔥 **HOT TIP:** You can use Google Maps to see what a place looks like before you visit.

10 Exploring free software

Introduction

You'll find a lot of free software on the internet, and some of it is good, valuable software. For instance, Microsoft Security Essentials is excellent security software you can trust, and OpenOffice is a great alternative to expensive office suite programs. Skype is safe, as are Picasa, Windows Live Messenger, AIM and hundreds of other titles.

However, there's a lot of bad software too; this is often software that simply doesn't work as advertised. Worse, some free software will infect your computer with malware or cause hard-to-diagnose computer problems. Thus, you have to be very careful about installing free software, and be vigilant not to fall for ruses. You have to make sure you never relinquish control of your computer to a rogue software program.

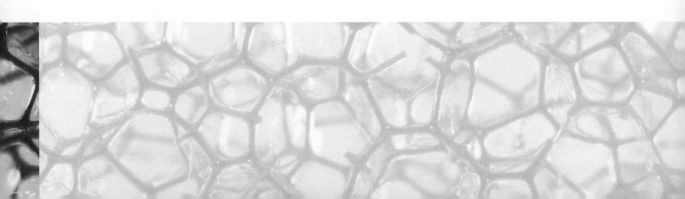

Don't install anything, yet!

It's important to read the first few pages of this chapter before you install any software you find on the internet. Here's why.

- Some free software is 'buggy'. This means it won't work properly and may cause computer-wide problems that you'll have to diagnose and fix.
- Companies often lure you in with a free trial, and then nag you forever to buy the full version.
- Some websites offer to fix problems for you (by installing a driver, for instance), but will often install spyware on your computer so they can track you on the internet.

Learn More

other threats before they reach your c

- Security software proven to stop onlin
- Won't slow down your computer or di and play.

FREE TRIAL   (Download size: 74.96 MB)

! ALERT: Security software companies often offer to scan your computer for free, and then claim to find a virus. Of course, they'll then encourage you to buy their program to get rid of it (often when no virus exists).

! ALERT: Never let a website run a scan of your computer to find problems, viruses or malware. You can be sure the site will find a problem (even if you don't have one) and want to charge you to fix it. Refer to the next section for more information.

Understand the ruse behind the 'free scan'

If you have even minor experience of the internet, you've probably seen the option to run a free scan to check your computer for viruses and malware, or to 'clean' your computer's Registry. There are many reasons why you should never do this.

- When you let a website run a scan of your computer, you often have to install software. This software can contain its own viruses, malware, spyware and the like.
- Companies that offer to scan your computer may place real viruses on it so they can be found.
- Scans may claim to find malware or other problems that don't actually exist. The company will then prompt you to purchase a program to get rid of what's not really there.
- When you install software from a company you don't know, you are risking your computer's security and your personal identity.

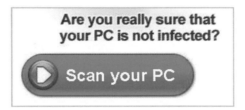

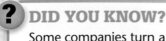 **DID YOU KNOW?**
Some companies turn a good profit by running free scans, finding fake viruses and charging people to remove them.

ALERT: Rogue scanning software can hijack your web browser so that you can only visit one site, the site where you can purchase the company's software, and you won't be able to access any other websites until you purchase the software from it (or take your computer to a computer repair shop).

Obtain free software safely

Now that you know a little about what to avoid when obtaining free software, you can begin to obtain it, provided you follow some simple guidelines.

1. Choose free programs approved by trusted websites, like CNet.com.

2. Research the program with a basic web search. Read comments posted by users.

3. Verify your security software is running and up to date.

4. Make sure you are getting the software from the company and not a third-party link.

5. During the acquisition process, make sure you're getting the free version of the software, and have not mistakenly opted for the paid version.

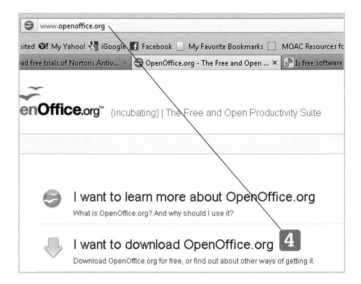

Explore the Microsoft Fix It Solution Center

When you have a computer problem, you probably look to the internet for a solution. You may find a solution you can apply, or you may be prompted to install a software program that can fix the problem for you. Both of these options are dangerous most of the time. If you're looking for a reliable solution to a Microsoft-related computer problem, visit the Microsoft Fix It Solution Center.

1 Visit www.support.microsoft.com/fixit.

2 Select the type of problem you're having.

3 Click Run Now if you see your specific problem in the results.

4 Accept any terms of use, give the required permissions, etc. as required.

ALERT: Don't choose the fix-it-for-me option on any other website!

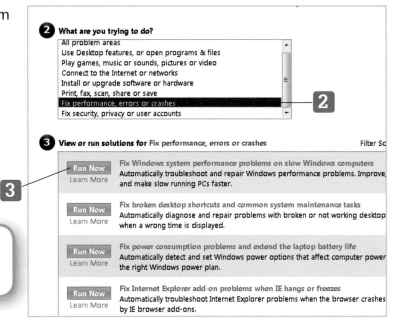

? DID YOU KNOW?

Microsoft offers free software too. You learned about Microsoft Security Essentials and the Malicious Software Removal Tool in Chapter 2. There are other free options from Microsoft, including free trials of their Microsoft Office software suite.

? DID YOU KNOW?

The Microsoft Fix It Solution Center can automatically fix problems with your computer, and you can trust it. That's not the case with most other 'fix-it-for-me' websites.

Explore Ad-Aware

Ad-Aware is a free, reliable and trusted adware prevention program from Lavasoft. You can see when you visit the company's website that the software has received rave reviews. The software claims to keep you safe from password stealers, keyloggers, virus, spyware, rootkits, trojans, online fraudsters, identity thieves and other potential cyber criminals.

1 Navigate to www.lavasoft.com.

2 Click Download Ad-Aware Free.

3 Click Download again.

4 Make sure, when prompted, you opt for the free version.

5 Follow the prompts to download and install the software.

2 ——— Download Ad-Aware FREE ⬇

 HOT TIP: Configure Ad-Aware to get definitions and updates automatically.

? DID YOU KNOW?

It's often advisable not to run multiple security programs, but Ad-Aware works to develop software that won't conflict with other running programs. If you install Ad-Aware and are prompted about other running programs, read the information and make a decision about which to use.

Explore OpenOffice

OpenOffice is free office software. It includes word processing, spreadsheet, email and presentation software that is compatible with the Microsoft Office suites. The software is reliable, and you can trust it. Make sure to download OpenOffice from the OpenOffice website though, and not through a third party.

1 Visit www.openoffice.org.

2 Locate the option to download the software.

3 Work through the download process.

4 Once installed, explore the programs as desired.

I want to download OpenOffice.org

Download OpenOffice.org for free, or find out about other ways of getting it.

Download now!

Start downloading OpenOffice.org 3.3.0 for Windows in English (US)
(Java Runtime Environment (JRE) included for all OS versions except Linux 32/64-bit Debian and Mac OS)

Get all platforms and languages | Release Notes | MD5 checksums | ISO images | order CD-ROM | P2P downloads

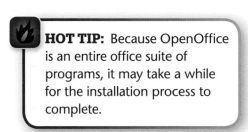

HOT TIP: Because OpenOffice is an entire office suite of programs, it may take a while for the installation process to complete.

WHAT DOES THIS MEAN?

Writer: this is the OpenOffice word processing program; it may be a good place to start since you're probably already familiar with other word processing programs.

Use Amazon's Kindle Cloud Reader

If you purchase digital books from Amazon, you can use their Kindle Cloud Reader to read those books on your computer or laptop.

1 From your computer, navigate to https://read.amazon.com.

2 Sign in.

3 Click Get Started Now, then click Allow.

4 Click any book to open it.

Set Up Kindle Cloud Reader for Offline Reading

Click the **"Allow"** button twice: once in the popup and once in the bar at the top of your browser window.

? DID YOU KNOW?

If you read part of a book on your Kindle device, and then opt to read at your computer (or vice versa), Amazon will know where you left off and will ask you if you'd like to go to the last page read.

🔥 HOT TIP: Use the left and right arrows that appear in a book to move among the pages, and click Library to return to your reading list.

Choose and use a messaging program

You might know how to send a text message from your phone to someone else's phone. This is a popular form of text messaging. You may not know that you can also send a text message from one computer to another computer, from a computer to a smartphone or tablet and vice versa. There are lots of programs to help you do this, and many are free and safe to install.

- Facebook offers messaging software called Messenger. Click Messages to get started.
- AOL has messaging software called AIM.
- Google offers Google Talk. This may be harder to set up and use than other options.
- Microsoft offers Windows Live Messenger. This is an older program and you may have several contacts that use it.

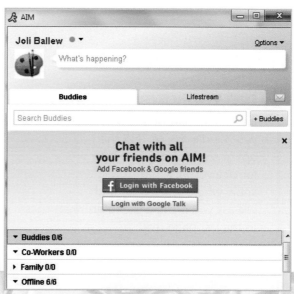

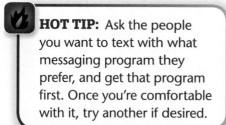

HOT TIP: Ask the people you want to text with what messaging program they prefer, and get that program first. Once you're comfortable with it, try another if desired.

? DID YOU KNOW?
Facebook Messenger is easy to use and doesn't require too much set up, and there's a Messenger app for smartphones and tablets. Messages sent through Messenger, from smartphones, aren't calculated as text messages by the phone company, instead they are calculated as data usage.

? DID YOU KNOW?
Many programs like AIM are compatible with other messaging programs like Facebook and Google Talk.

Find more free software you can trust

Earlier in this chapter you learned about some of the more popular free software, including OpenOffice and Ad-Aware. There are a lot more titles to choose from though. There's Picasa for photo management and sharing, Skype for video conferencing, Mozilla Thunderbird for email and GIMP for photo editing, to name a few. But how can you know what you can trust and what you can't?

- Know that you can trust established companies like PC Magazine, CNet and PC World to give you unbiased and truthful reviews of software.
- Review lists of software downloaded the most.
- Read the reviews of any software you think you'd like to use before you download it.
- Access the download option from the website that created the software, and not from a third-party site.
- Follow all other advice offered in this chapter and this book.

Most Popular Downloads

Downloads for last week

1.	AVG Anti-Virus Free Edition 2012	1,034,985
2.	Avast Free Antivirus	778,123
3.	Malwarebytes Anti-Malware	509,531
4.	Advanced SystemCare Free	478,630
5.	WinRAR (32-bit)	413,461
6.	Avira Free Antivirus	344,622
7.	TeamViewer	344,408
8.	Internet Download Manager	297,805
9.	CNET TechTracker	286,932
10.	Free YouTube Downloader	252,555
11.	Virtual DJ	246,242
12.	Google Chrome	221,326
13.	MyVideoConverter	214,820
14.	Camfrog Video Chat	210,364
15.	GOM Media Player	209,824
16.	VLC Media Player	193,151
17.	Adobe Flash Player	192,696

 ALERT: Do more than just read the information on websites that offer testimonials of their software; always refer to independent reviews too.

Be careful with free trials

Many legitimate websites offer free trials of software. Even if the free trials don't contain adware or spyware, there are still inherent problems.

- Once the free trial period is over, the program may still prompt you to buy the full version in the form of pop-ups.
- The program may open when you double-click a picture, word document, song, audiobook or other data, even though you won't be able to view the data without purchasing the program.
- The program is taking up hard drive space; this can be a problem if your hard drive is running low on space.
- The program may be tying up system resources by running without your knowledge in the background.

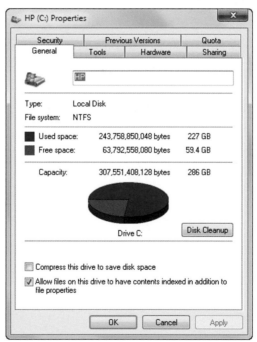

HOT TIP: On a Windows 7 computer you can view the software currently running (or running in the background) from the Notification area of the Taskbar.

SEE ALSO: 'Uninstall unwanted software', next.

Uninstall unwanted software

You should always uninstall software you no longer want to use. This prevents programs from running in the background without your knowledge, from taking up hard drive space and from prompting you to buy the software or get updates. Here's how to uninstall a program using Windows 7:

1 Click Start and click Control Panel.

2 Click Uninstall a program.

3 Locate the program to uninstall and click it once.

4 Click Uninstall/Change.

5 Work through the prompts to uninstall the program.

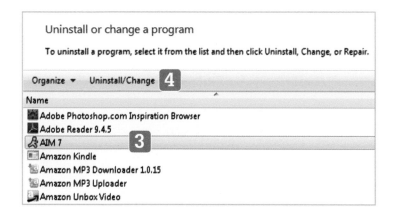

ALERT: When uninstalling programs, never uninstall something you don't recognise. You just may need it.

HOT TIP: Uninstall unwanted toolbars, messaging programs, software (both free and paid) and software for hardware you no longer own or use.

11 Keeping children and grandchildren safe

Introduction

Protecting your children and grandchildren while they are surfing the internet is a complex task. You have to explain the possible dangers clearly, create a limited computer user account for them, and depending on their age, set parental controls and monitor their web activities. At the very least you have to enable any available 'safe search' features, uninstall (or make unavailable) any web browsers you can't lock down, and possibly even install software like Windows Live Family Safety. No matter what you configure though, if the children are computer-savvy, they will learn how to bypass the controls you've put in place eventually. Protecting minors on the internet is thus an ongoing task.

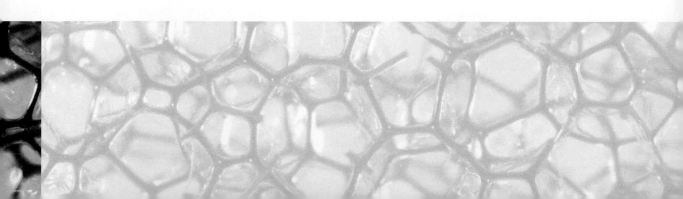

8 Click OK.

9 Back at the main parental controls screen, click Games.

10 Explore the games settings, including limiting games based on their ratings. Click OK.

11 Repeat to explore Time Limits.

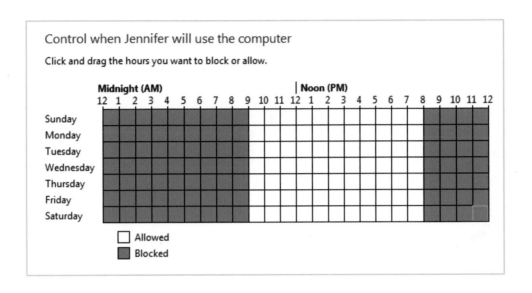

Control when Jennifer will use the computer

Click and drag the hours you want to block or allow.

☐ Allowed
■ Blocked

 DID YOU KNOW?

When you set time limits for a standard user account, that user cannot log on to the computer during hours you've blocked. If they can't log on, and you've logged off, they can't access the internet.

HOT TIP: Parental Controls in Windows 7 affect the entire computer, not just internet-related tasks.

? **DID YOU KNOW?**

Software is available that you can purchase, such as SafeChat and NetNanny. Generally you install the software, let the software know which user you want to protect (or limit), and you work through the set-up process. This software will then generate reports you can view that include usage data, attempts to bypass controls and more.

Consider free software like Windows Live Family Safety

If creating a standard user account, configuring content filters, setting parental controls and the like doesn't achieve what you need to achieve with a child, you can try Windows Live Family Safety. It's free and part of the Windows Live Essentials suite available from http://explore.live.com. Click Essentials, and look for 'Other Programs'.

- Family Safety enhances the parental controls already available on Windows computers.
- Settings can be managed from any computer, so you don't have to log on to the child's computer.
- Reports are generated and easy to read.
- You can block inappropriate content easily.

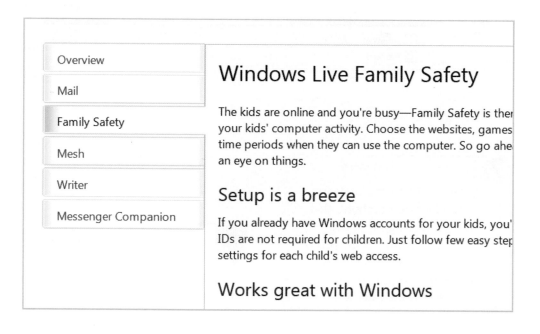

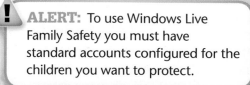

ALERT: To use Windows Live Family Safety you must have standard accounts configured for the children you want to protect.

ALERT: Make sure you obtain any Microsoft programs from Microsoft's website and not a third-party website.

Educate yourself about the sites children visit

You can learn which sites the children, tweens or teens you're responsible for visit the most by asking them. Often they will be happy to tell you if you sound interested; then you can visit those sites yourself to see what they are all about. Checking in on their history every now and then isn't a bad idea either. Here's how to do that in Internet Explorer 9. Other web browsers are similar.

1 Click Tools, then Explorer Bars, then History.

2 Click any option to expand it.

3 Now, click the arrow by View by Date, and select View By Most Visited.

4 Explore the sites listed.

5 Explore other sorting options.

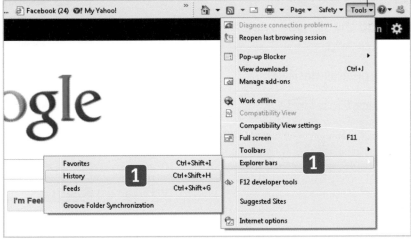

WHAT DOES THIS MEAN?

History list: this is a list of sites the user has visited over the past three weeks.

? DID YOU KNOW?

Change the setting to Search History to search for a website by name.

Modify the list of blocked websites

If, despite your best efforts, a child is still visiting specific websites you don't want him or her too, you can block access to the site manually. How you do this depends on the web browser you've chosen to use. Because Internet Explorer is the most popular browser at present, in this example you'll learn to add a website to this browser's Blocked Sites list.

1 In Internet Explorer, click Tools and Internet Options.

2 Click the Security tab.

3 Click Restricted sites.

4 Click Sites.

5 Add the site you want to block and click Add.

6 Repeat as desired.

7 Click Close and OK.

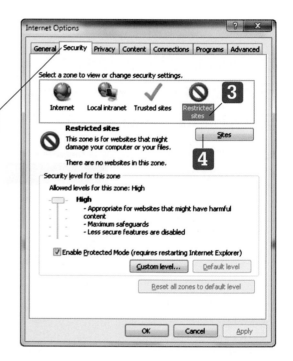

HOT TIP: Try to access the sites you've blocked to verify the settings.

ALERT: Remember, if you block sites in Internet Explorer but leave Google Chrome, Apple's Safari or Mozilla Firefox installed and available, a child can still access those sites using those browsers.

12 Dealing with cyberbullying, cybercrime and cyberstalking

Introduction

Close to half of all school children report being bullied online at least once; your children or grandchildren may already be victims. Almost all adults have been a victim of some type of cybercrime (identity theft, fraudulent or phishing emails in your inbox, and computer intrusions such as viruses and malware). Additionally, reports of cyberstalking are on the rise; victims are harassed online, an act which sometimes leads to physical stalking. There are ways to deal with this, from avoidance to alerting the authorities to suspending all online activities until the threat is neutralised.

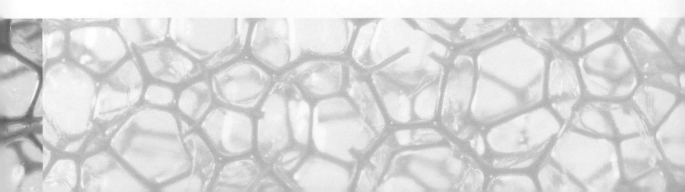

Understand the threats

In this chapter you'll learn how to deal with three of the most common personal, online threats. If you ever become a victim, refer to this chapter to document, report and defuse the situation as quickly as possible.

- Cyberbullying – this generally occurs with children and teens, and they bully others for the usual reasons (to prove they are tough, to intimidate or instill fear).
- Cybercrime – most of the time, cybercrime is online identity theft. In more general terms, it's any crime that's committed using a computer and the internet.
- Cyberstalking – cyberstalkers seek to instill fear, and to harass, embarrass and humiliate their victims.

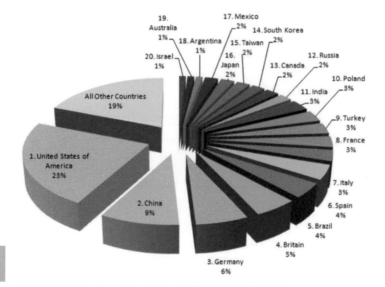

Cybercrime: Top 20 countries

 DID YOU KNOW?

Cyberbullies use online tools to achieve their goals, including deprecating users on social networks, sending threatening email, sending harassing phone texts and slandering the user in online chats and groups.

! ALERT: Initial acts of online cyberstalking may escalate into attempts to damage a person's credit score, ruin relationships with family members, bosses and coworkers, and, in general, damage one's online reputation.

HOT TIP: Personal attacks by cyberbullies and cyberstalkers often start because someone gets angry or feels slighted. You can often diffuse a situation by apologising, even if you're sure you are in the right.

Know what to do first when problems begin

Once you know a problem exists, there are a few things you should do immediately. Here are some tips you can employ whether or not you know your harasser:

- Apologise if you know the person and think it might help.
- If an apology doesn't work, stop all communication. Ignore them.
- Never communicate with people you suspect are trying to scam you.
- Create a rule to send automatically all email from the harasser, criminal or bully to a specific folder.
- Hide or block anything the harasser posts to your social networking website. However, if you think the problem will escalate, take a screenshot of the post first.
- Do anything else possible to avoid, diffuse or minimise the situation, including contacting parents or bosses, as applicable.

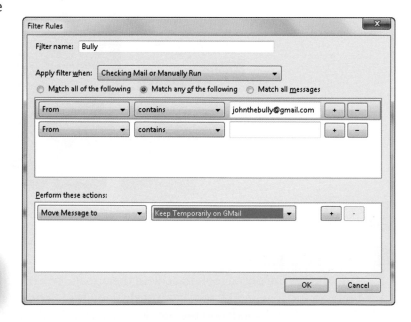

▶ **SEE ALSO:** 'Record online attacks', next.

HOT TIP: It's important to save and document threatening emails and posts, because the problem may escalate. If you have to, you can forward those messages to a headteacher or the police.

? **DID YOU KNOW?**
Often an apology works to diffuse a situation, even if you don't mean it.

Record online attacks

If you've apologised, ignored, talked to a bully's parents and otherwise done your best to separate yourself from your bully, criminal or stalker (even if you don't know who it is), you must begin the process of actively recording all online attacks. One way is to take a screenshot of a webpage where the threat is posted. Here's how to take a screenshot on a Windows-based computer.

1 Navigate to the webpage where the threat is posted.

2 Press the Print Screen (or PRT SCR) button on the keyboard.

3 Open any program that enables you to 'paste' what you've copied.

4 Click Paste.

5 Save the file.

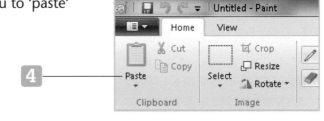

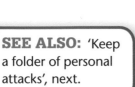

SEE ALSO: 'Keep a folder of personal attacks', next.

? DID YOU KNOW?
If you can't find the Paste command, try using the keyboard shortcut Ctrl + V.

? DID YOU KNOW?
You can forward threatening emails to a friend for safe keeping.

Keep a folder of personal attacks

If you think you'll eventually have to report a person or anonymous criminal to the police, create a folder that contains the information you've amassed. Here's how to create a folder on a Windows-based computer and move a screenshot of a webpage there.

1 Right-click an empty area of the Desktop and click New, then Folder.

2 Name the folder as desired.

3 Position the new folder so you can see both it and the saved file.

4 Left-click the file, drag it to the folder, and drop it there.

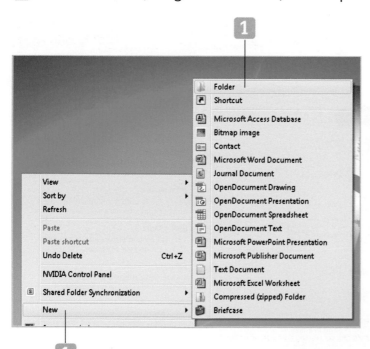

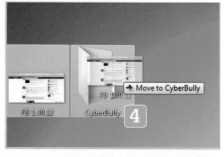

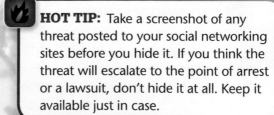

? DID YOU KNOW?
You can save an email to a folder too. Click the email, click File and Save As (if that feature is available), and choose the folder to save it to.

HOT TIP: Take a screenshot of any threat posted to your social networking sites before you hide it. If you think the threat will escalate to the point of arrest or a lawsuit, don't hide it at all. Keep it available just in case.

Print what you can

If you receive any threats via your computer, you can often print them. You may be able to print email, blog posts, web pages, chat transcripts and more. Look for the print option.

1 In email programs, look under the File menu for a print command.

2 In web browsers, look under the File menu. If you don't see any menus, press the Alt key on the keyboard.

3 In messaging programs, enable options to record all chats. You can print recorded chats.

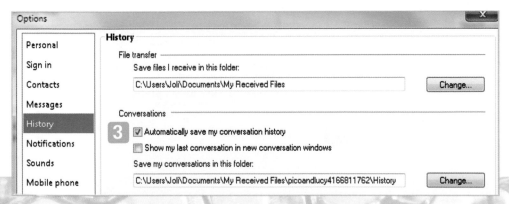

ALERT: Do not reply to chats or instant messages sent by bullies or stalkers.

HOT TIP: Before approaching the authorities, gather as much information as possible, and include duplicates (print data and digital data).

Report a cyberbully

If you, your child, spouse or a partner, sibling or grandchildren are being bullied online, gather your data first. Write down the resolution you want. Be specific. Then:

1 If there's an online form for reporting bullies, use it.

2 Report bullying to parents, headteachers, school administrators, bosses, etc. as applicable.

3 If school administrators or bosses don't resolve the problem, contact the school board, Human Resources department or next higher authority.

4 Inform whoever you tell that if they can't resolve the problem in a reasonable amount of time, you'll continue to move up the chain of command.

5 Report the bullying to a CEO, company owner, school superintendent or college dean.

6 Report bullying to the police.

7 If the local police can't resolve your problem, look elsewhere (private detective, solicitor, etc.)

Bully Prevention and Reporting

The School Board is committed to providing an educational setting that is safe, secure, and free from harassment and bullying for all of its students and school employees. The District will not tolerate unlawful bullying and harassment of any type.

The District in consultation with District students, parents, teachers, administrators, school staff, school volunteers, community representatives, and local law enforcement agencies have developed a District policy as part of a comprehensive plan intended to prevent bullying and harassment. Download District's Policy on Bullying and Harassment. English | Spanish

A reporting system has been created to appropriately identify, report, investigate, and respond to situations of bullying and harassment. Click here for online form to report a bully.

The District has also created this website as a resource and tool to help cultivate a learning environment where everyone involved can thrive and achieve excellence in education.

1 Click here to report a bully.

 HOT TIP: If you can identify the bully, harasser or criminal, often a well-written letter from a solicitor will put a halt to it.

! ALERT: Document everything that happens with every person you report to. Document what they did or did not do to resolve the problem; document the outcome (or lack of one). Take this information to the next higher authority when necessary.

! ALERT: Some people you'll contact won't have any tools at their disposal to deal with your situation, and the police may have to be involved sooner than later.

Report cyber crime

As with any other online threat, gather your data first. This may involve printing emails or chat transcripts, saving and printing online threats, and so on. Then:

1. Using the internet, search for where to report cybercrimes in your area.

2. Look for links that will take you to a place to report the crime.

3. If there's no online form, contact the police or visit the local cybercrime office.

4. Fill out the required information, and print the webpage if you can.

5. If you can't print your report, take a screenshot using Print Screen.

6. If you don't get a response or the issue is not resolved, continue to work your way up any chain of command.

Hot Documents

2

- **How to Report Cyber and IP Crime**
  - How to Report Computer- and Internet- Related Crime
  - How to Report Intellectual Property Crime

ALERT: If you are in immediate danger, always call the police first.

ALERT: Often cybercrimes can't be solved by your local police, bank or government entity. You may have to enlist a solicitor, credit agency or private detective for help.

? DID YOU KNOW? Sometimes you know exactly what crime was committed. Perhaps your bank account was compromised. In this case, contact the bank first.

Report cyberstalking

Cyberstalking is extremely dangerous. You should report stalking to the police immediately. That's because cyberstalking often escalates to physical stalking. It's not hard for a determined stalker to find out where you live, work, play or socialise.

- Learn everything you can about cyberstalking.
- Record everything, and record it daily.
- Keep a journal.
- Contact the police even if you don't know your stalker.
- Inform neighbours, friends and family members.
- Press charges.

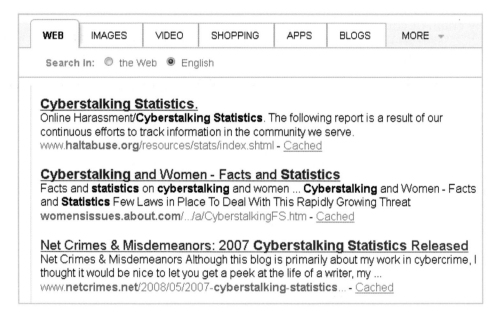

 **DID YOU KNOW?**
Most victims of cyberstalkers are women between the ages of 18 and 29.

ALERT: Stalking and domestic violence go hand in hand. Do what you need to do to get away from a stalker.

Change your email address, user names and passwords

If you've been a victim of a bully, stalker or criminal, it's best to make some changes to your online identity, starting with creating a new email address. This is especially important if you've had your identity stolen. You should follow that with new user names and passwords for all of the websites you log in to. Although making these changes is time-consuming, it's worth it.

- Monitor the email you get, and make a note of the people you communicate with regularly and trust.
- Inform only those people of your new email address, and ask them not to share it.
- Create a disposable email address for social networking websites.
- Visit every website you've ever logged in to and change your current user name and password to something new.
- Delete accounts for websites, including social networking sites, that you no longer use.

Tweet privacy	☐ Protect my Tweets
	Only let people whom I approve follow my Tweets. If this is checked, your future Tweets will not be available publicly. Tweets posted previously may still be publicly visible in some places.
HTTPS only	☑ Always use HTTPS
	Use a secure connection where possible.
Country	United States ▼
	Select your country. This setting is saved to this browser.

Save changes

Deactivate my account

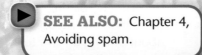

SEE ALSO: Chapter 4, Avoiding spam.

Change or suspend social networking accounts

If the police can't catch a cyberstalker, and you are still afraid, harassed and fearful, you can suspend accounts at social networking websites, stop posting to your blog, and otherwise make yourself unavailable for online harassment. Although this is a drastic measure, it will prevent a stalker from contacting you using this medium (or at least you won't see when he or she does).

1 Log in to any site you use and want to suspend.

2 Locate the Account options.

3 Locate any option to deactivate or suspend your account.

ALERT: If a school or company refuses to work with you to resolve a problem, contact a solicitor. There are laws in place to protect you from online crimes and harassment.

? DID YOU KNOW?
Sometimes a cyberstalker will get bored and move on to other prey. Suspending your social networking account may be just what the doctor ordered!

ALERT: If you've done everything outlined in this chapter but you are still being victimised, continue to document and report each incident to the police, HR department, parent, headteacher and so on. It may take more than one report to convince them you're serious about putting an end to it.

13 Securing your computer and network

Introduction

You know you must secure your computer with security software to protect yourself and your data from online threats. You know to create complex passwords and to store those passwords in a safe place, to keep people from hacking into your online accounts. You know how to get yourself out of trouble when you get in it! In fact, if you've read this entire book, you're armed with at least a hundred ways to protect yourself and your computer from online dangers.

In this chapter you'll learn a few techniques for securing your Windows-based computer and your home network that have yet to be introduced (or perhaps bear repeating). Some are easy, like logging off from your password-protected computer account when you've finished using it, while others require a little more work, like verifying your Wi-Fi network is secure.

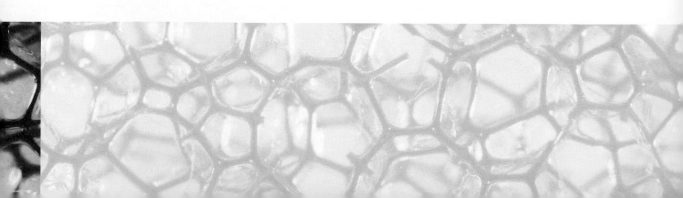

Log off or lock your computer

When you sit down at your computer you probably open your email program, log in to Facebook or LinkedIn, open folders that contain your personal files and so on. If you walk away from your computer without logging off or locking it, anyone can sit down in front of it and access both your online data and personal data stored on your computer. You should always log off or lock the computer when you're going to move away from it.

1 On a Windows-based computer, click the Start button.

2 Click the right-arrow shown here.

3 Click Lock or Log off.

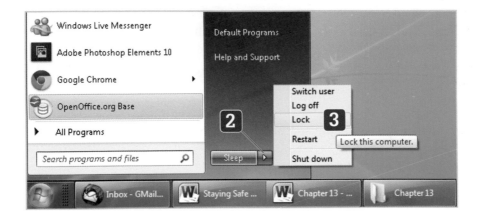

HOT TIP: Hopefully you've followed the advice in this book and created password-protected user accounts for everyone you want to have access to your computer. If you haven't done that, refer to Chapter 11 to learn how.

? DID YOU KNOW?
It's faster to get back to work if you choose Lock vs. Log off.

WHAT DOES THIS MEAN?

Log off: when you *log off* your computer, you make it available for someone else to log on to it.

Lock: when you *lock* the computer you leave programs and files open, but enable the lock screen. Either way, if your account is password-protected, you must type the password to gain access again.

Check for and resolve security issues

Windows 7 computers offer a unique way to check for and resolve security issues through the Action Center. Most problems identified in the Action Center also come with a suggestion to fix the problem.

1 Click Start, and click Control Panel.

2 In Category view, shown here, click Review your computer's status.

3 Review any issues shown in red or yellow as well as their solutions.

4 Apply solutions as applicable.

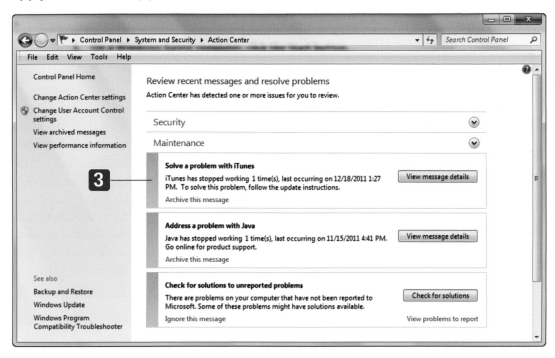

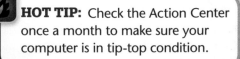 **HOT TIP:** Check the Action Center once a month to make sure your computer is in tip-top condition.

ALERT: If you see a pop-up appear on your screen and you aren't sure if it originated from the Action Center, don't click it! Instead, open the Action Center to see if anything needs attention.

Find and fix problems

Windows 7 computers also offer a way to find and fix problems using the Control Panel. It's best to fix problems as you become aware of them, because many problems can cause security breaches.

1 Click Start, and click Control Panel.

2 In Category view, click Find and fix problems.

3 Select the category that describes the problem you're having.

4 Work through the wizard as prompted to resolve problems.

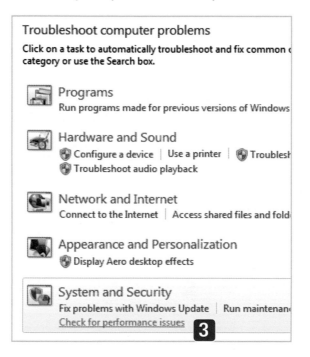

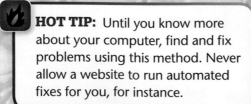 **HOT TIP:** Until you know more about your computer, find and fix problems using this method. Never allow a website to run automated fixes for you, for instance.

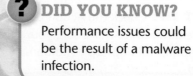 **DID YOU KNOW?**
Performance issues could be the result of a malware infection.

Change administrator accounts to standard accounts

As you learned in Chapter 11, Windows computers offer two kinds of user accounts. There are Administrator accounts which give the user complete control over the system as well as the ability to install programs, and there are Standard accounts, which are much more limited and do not allow users to perform installations (among other things). Review the accounts configured on your computer, and change any unnecessary Administrator accounts to Standard accounts.

1 Click Start, and click Control Panel.

2 Click Add or remove user accounts.

3 Click the Administrator account to demote.

4 Click Change the account type.

5 Click Standard user and then, Change Account Type.

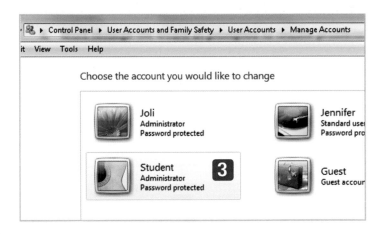

ALERT: If a virus or other pieces of malware tries to install while a standard user is logged on, that user may be prompted to provide an administrator name and password to allow it.

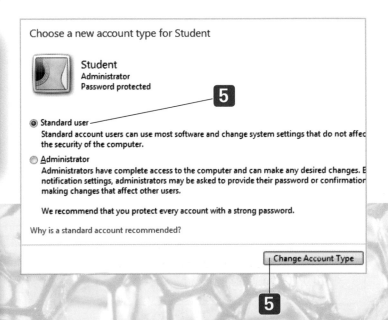

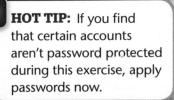

HOT TIP: If you find that certain accounts aren't password protected during this exercise, apply passwords now.

Keep your operating system up to date

All versions of Windows computers offer a feature called Windows Update. It should be configured to get and install updates automatically and on a schedule.

1 Click Start and click All Programs.

2 Click Windows Update.

3 If you see something other than a green tick mark, as shown here, click Change settings and enable Windows Update to run on a schedule.

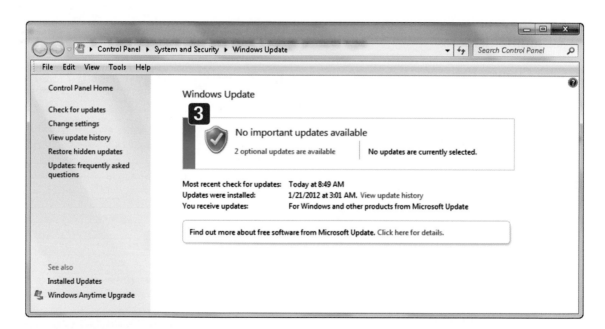

WHAT DOES THIS MEAN?

An update: often contains files that help secure your computer.

? DID YOU KNOW?

Microsoft may send updates as often as once or twice a week. When you get a new computer, you may be asked to update your system a dozen times or more!

Check for optional updates

If Windows Update is set optimally, all recommended, important and critical updates will be installed automatically. Optional updates will not. Sometimes you'll find that optional updates are available, though. You should review these and install them if they pertain to you.

1 Open Windows Update as outlined in the previous section.

2 If you see that optional updates are available, click the notification.

3 Review the updates.

4 If desired, install the updates.

? DID YOU KNOW?

The old adage 'If it ain't broke don't fix it' doesn't apply to Windows Update. If you see that a recommended, important or critical update is available, install it.

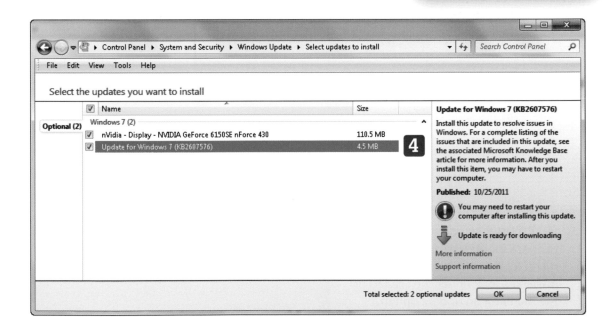

HOT TIP: Your computer checks for updates in the middle of the night, by default. If your computer is not on or connected to the internet at that time, it will check for updates the next time it is.

ALERT: Sometimes optional updates include 'language packs'. You do not need to install these optional updates unless they apply to you directly.

Keep programs up to date

Windows 7 is an operating system. You keep the operating system up to date with Windows Update. Programs are software you install in addition to the operating system. Microsoft Office, Skype, Windows Live Messenger, Photoshop Elements 10 and similar software are programs. You have to keep programs up to date too.

1 Open any program you use often.

2 Click the Help menu.

3 Click Check for updates, or something similar.

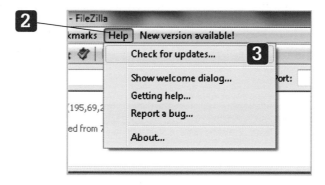

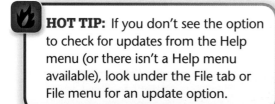

HOT TIP: If you don't see the option to check for updates from the Help menu (or there isn't a Help menu available), look under the File tab or File menu for an update option.

? DID YOU KNOW?

Most programs offer a Help menu, and from that menu, an option to check for updates.

! ALERT: You may be prompted to pay for updates but generally you don't need to do this. In these cases you're buying an 'upgrade' to the program which contains new features, and won't get the type of (generally security) update we're talking about here.

Keep your web browser up to date

Updates are often sent automatically to your web browser to increase security. Although updates should be applied automatically, depending on the browser, you may be able to check for updates manually.

- Updates to Internet Explorer are part of Windows Update.
- In Firefox, click Help and About Firefox to learn about updates.
- You can manually check for updates to Safari on a Mac from the Apple menu. For Windows computers, you'll be prompted when an update is available.
- Chrome is configured to get updates automatically. However, if you see a green arrow on the wrench icon, an update is available and has not been applied.

.

 HOT TIP: Strive to use the latest version of the web browser you prefer. As an example, if you like Internet Explorer 9 and notice that Internet Explorer 10 is available, get it. New web browsers are generally more secure and offer more features than their predecessors.

 DID YOU KNOW?
Most web browsers are preconfigured to get updates automatically, without intervention from you.

HOT TIP: When prompted to restart your computer after an update is applied, do so. Don't wait!

Verify your Wi-Fi network is password protected

If you have a wireless network in your home, it should be protected by a password. You configure the password using the settings available from your router manufacturer. If you aren't sure if your wireless network is protected, you can check fairly easily. One way is to invite someone to your home and see if they can connect:

1 Invite a friend to your home.

2 Ask them to bring their smart phone, iPad, Kindle Fire, laptop or other device with Wi-Fi capabilities.

3 Have them enable Wi-Fi features.

4 Have them check for a Wi-Fi network.

5 When they find yours, ask them to join it. A lock icon implies it's protected.

6 If they are prompted for a password, your network is protected.

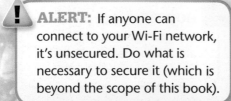 **ALERT:** If anyone can connect to your Wi-Fi network, it's unsecured. Do what is necessary to secure it (which is beyond the scope of this book).

 HOT TIP: There are other ways to check to see if your Wi-Fi network is secure, but this one is more fun than the others!

Top 10 Staying Safe Online Problems Solved

Problem 1: My computer is acting strangely, but it's not a virus!

If your computer is acting strangely, and you've already run a scan of your system using your security software, the problem is elsewhere. Windows 7 computers offer a way to find and fix problems using Control Panel. If you know of a problem, use this technique to fix it.

1 Click Start, and click Control Panel.

2 In Category view, click Find and fix problems.

3 Select the category that describes the problem you're having.

4 Work through the wizard as prompted to resolve problems.

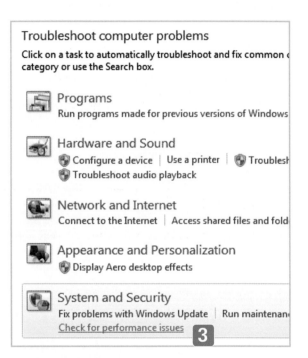

Troubleshoot computer problems

Click on a task to automatically troubleshoot and fix common category or use the Search box.

Programs
Run programs made for previous versions of Windows

Hardware and Sound
Configure a device | Use a printer | Troublesh
Troubleshoot audio playback

Network and Internet
Connect to the Internet | Access shared files and fold

Appearance and Personalization
Display Aero desktop effects

System and Security
Fix problems with Windows Update | Run maintenan
Check for performance issues

 HOT TIP: Until you know more about your computer, find and fix problems using this method. Never allow a website to run automated fixes for you, for instance.

? DID YOU KNOW?
Performance issues could be the result of a malware infection.

Problem 2: I created an account for my grandchild but he keeps logging on to mine!

If you create a limited or standard user account for a child and apply parental controls or other limitations, but you leave your account open (not password-protected) or don't log off or lock the computer when you're finished using it, that child will learn pretty quickly that he can access the computer through your account and do whatever he wants! Thus, it is imperative that all user accounts on your computer have passwords.

1 On a Windows-based computer, open Control Panel.

2 Click Add or remove user accounts.

3 Click any account that is not currently password-protected.

4 Click Create a password.

5 Fill in the required information and click Create password.

6 Repeat for all accounts that do not have a password applied.

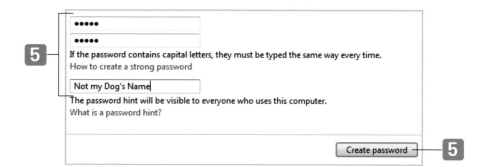

? DID YOU KNOW?
You can create password-protected accounts on Apple and Linux machines; in this book though, we generally detail steps for Windows-based computers.

! ALERT: During this exercise, make sure the Guest account is turned off.

Problem 3: My child is being bullied online. How do I report it?

If you, your child, spouse or partner, sibling or grandchildren are being bullied online, gather your data first. Write down the resolution you want. Be specific. Then:

1 If there's an online form for reporting bullies, use it.

2 Report bullying to parents, headteachers, school administrators, bosses, etc. as applicable.

3 If school administrators or bosses don't resolve the problem, contact the school board, Human Resources department or next higher authority.

4 Inform whoever you tell that if they can't resolve the problem in a reasonable amount of time, you'll continue to move up the chain of command.

5 Report the bullying to a CEO, company owner, school superintendent or college dean.

6 Report bullying to the police.

7 If the local police can't resolve your problem, look elsewhere (private detective, solicitor, etc.)

Bully Prevention and Reporting

The School Board is committed to providing an educational setting that is safe, secure, and free from harassment and bullying for all of its students and school employees. The District will not tolerate unlawful bullying and harassment of any type.

The District in consultation with District students, parents, teachers, administrators, school staff, school volunteers, community representatives, and local law enforcement agencies have developed a District policy as part of a comprehensive plan intended to prevent bullying and harassment. Download District's Policy on Bullying and Harassment. English | Spanish

A reporting system has been created to appropriately identify, report, investigate, and respond to situations of bullying and harassment. Click here for online form to report a bully.

The District has also created this website as a resource and tool to help cultivate a learning environment where everyone involved can thrive and achieve excellence in education.

  Click here to report a bully.

 HOT TIP: If you can identify the bully, harasser or criminal, often a well-written letter from a solicitor will put a halt to it.

! ALERT: Document everything that happens with every person you report to. Document what they did or did not do to resolve the problem; document the outcome (or lack of one). Take this information to the next higher authority when necessary.

! ALERT: Some people you contact won't have any tools at their disposal to deal with your situation, and the police may have to be involved sooner rather than later.

Problem 4: How can I best protect my computer from viruses and other malware?

You must protect your computer from viruses. You can acquire viruses from email, from websites or even from office documents that contain macros (computer code that automates tasks). There's no way to avoid viruses forever, no matter how careful you are. You *must* install anti-virus software.

1 Purchase or download anti-virus software. Consider Microsoft Security Essentials, shown here.

2 Follow the instructions to install that software.

3 When prompted, configure the software to get updates regularly, if possible, each night.

WHAT DOES THIS MEAN?

Virus: A virus is harmful computer code that can cause your computer to act erratically, send out email as you, post to social networks as you, and spread to other computers without your knowledge.

4 Configure the software to run scans regularly too.

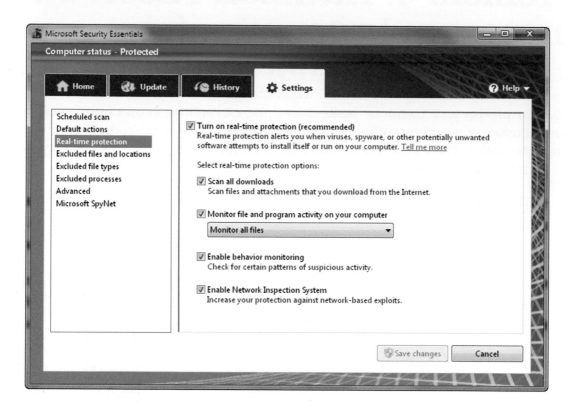

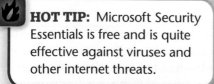 **HOT TIP:** Microsoft Security Essentials is free and is quite effective against viruses and other internet threats.

ALERT: Never install anti-virus software from a company you've never heard of! Likewise, never run free virus scans. Most of these 'companies' will place viruses (real or fake) on your computer and urge you to purchase their software to rid the computer of them.

Problem 5: I want to report an unsafe website

Browsers often offer a place to report an unsafe website. The option, if available, usually appears with the phishing options outlined in the previous section. As an example, here's how to report an unsafe website using Internet Explorer 9. Do this only if you are at the website you believe is fraudulent or a threat.

1 Click Safety.

2 Click SmartScreen Filter.

3 Click Report unsafe website.

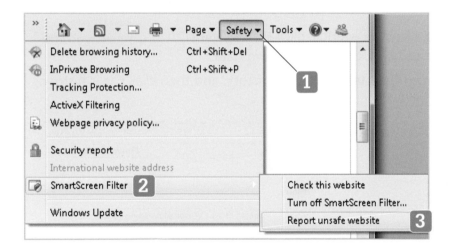

 HOT TIP: If you visit a website that is fraudulent and mimicking a real site (perhaps your bank or mortgage company), report the site to the institution being mimicked. Do this even if you can locate the option to report the site via your web browser.

? DID YOU KNOW?

In Firefox, click Help and Report Web Forgery to report a fraudulent website.

? DID YOU KNOW?

In Firefox you can click Tools and then Page Info to learn more about the web page you're visiting, including how many times you've visited it in the past. You can assume if you've visited the page often, it's the actual site where you pay your bill, do your banking or access other data.

Problem 6: I've been shopping for presents and need to delete my browsing history

All web browsers keep track of the websites you've visited. How long that data is kept depends on the browser, but it is often around three weeks. If you share a computer with someone and you don't want them to see the websites you've recently visited, you can delete your browsing history.

- In Internet Explorer, click Safety, then delete browsing history.
- In Firefox, click Tools, and then Clear recent history.
- In Chrome, click the wrench, click History, click Edit Items, and click Clear all browsing data.
- In Safari, from the Menu bar, click History, and then click Clear history.

HOT TIP: To show the Menu bar in Safari, Internet Explorer or Firefox, tap the Alt key on the keyboard.

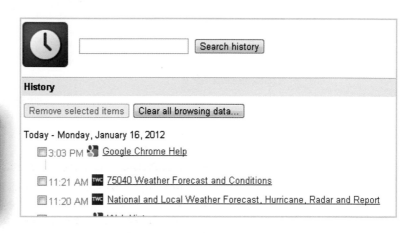

? DID YOU KNOW?

Grandchildren often know how to access the browsing history on a computer, and can figure out where you've been shopping and what you may have bought them for their birthday or Christmas!

? DID YOU KNOW?

You can configure almost any web browser so that no history is ever saved. In Safari, for instance, you configure this from Settings, Preferences, and the General tab.

Problem 7: How can I be sure that I can trust a website with my credit card information?

Before you make purchases from any website, make sure that the site can be trusted with your credit card information and other personal data. You can check easily by looking for https:// in the address bar. If you don't see the 's', don't enter any personal data.

1 When you're ready to make a purchase, note what is listed in the Address bar of your web browser window.

2 If you see https://, shown here, it's okay to make the purchase.

3 If you only see http://, do not enter any personal information.

 HOT TIP: Many websites now let you pay with PayPal, a secure way to perform online transactions. Setting up a PayPal account takes a little time, but you only have to do it once!

ALERT: Before you make purchases from a person on eBay or a similar website, make sure that person has good reviews and has been doing business at the site for a good amount of time.

? DID YOU KNOW?

The s after https means the website has taken steps to get a 'certificate' from a certificate authority, and that authority has deemed the site safe for handling your personal information.

Problem 8: I think my computer has a virus. What can I do?

If you suspect you have a security problem, you can run checks for viruses and malware. Use your security software to do this. If you don't have any security software, you'll use Windows Defender, detailed in Chapter 2.

1 Open your security software program.

2 Verify that it's up-to-date.

3 Look for an option to scan the computer.

4 Click Scan Now, or something similar.

5 If prompted, delete or quarantine threats found.

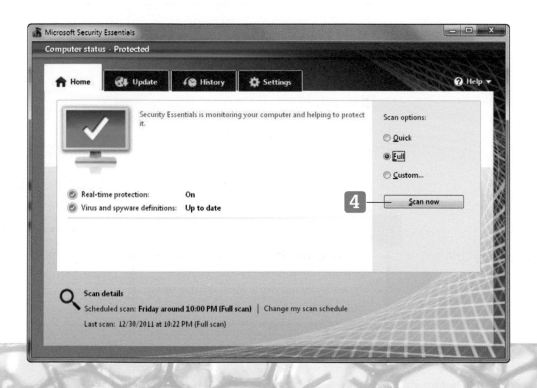

Problem 9: When I visit websites, I have to close a lot of pop-up ads

All of the popular web browsers come with a pop-up blocker that is enabled by default. If you're seeing pop-ups, it somehow became disabled. Here's how to access the pop-up settings in Internet Explorer and Firefox, and other browsers are similar.

1 In Internet Explorer:

  a Click Tools.

  b Click Pop-up Blocker.

  c Verify the pop-up blocker is enabled.

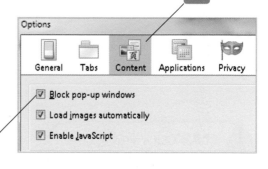

2 In Firefox:

  a Click Tools then Options.

  b Click the Content tab.

  c Verify that Block pop-up windows is enabled.

? DID YOU KNOW?

Other web browsers allow you to verify that pop-ups are blocked too. If you can't find the setting, search the web for 'block pop-ups in' followed by the name of your web browser.

? DID YOU KNOW?

Sometimes you need to allow a pop-up for a site. If this is the case, hold down the Alt key when clicking the link that produces a pop-up.

Problem 10: My child installed software I didn't approve of. How can I prevent this in future?

Only users with administrator accounts can install software. Thus, if a child is installing software you must change the account type from Administrator to Standard. Standard users can't install software without an administrator's permission (and password).

1 Click Start, and click Control Panel.

2 Click Add or remove user accounts.

3 Click the Administrator account to demote.

4 Click Change the account type.

5 Click Standard user and then, Change Account Type.

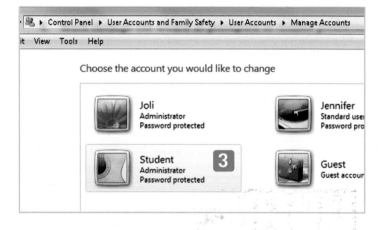

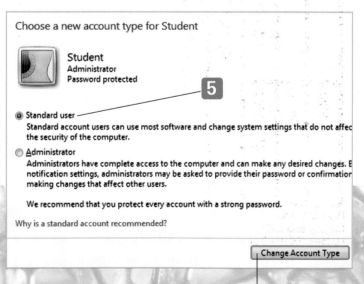

> ⚠ **ALERT:** If a virus or other pieces of malware tries to install while a standard user is logged on, that user may be prompted to provide an administrator name and password to allow it.

MOVEMENTS IN MODERN ART

FUTURISM

RICHARD HUMPHREYS

TATE PUBLISHING

First published 1999 by order of the Tate Trustees
by Tate Publishing, a division of Tate Enterprises
Ltd, Millbank, London SW1P 4RG
www.tate.org.uk

Reprinted 2003, 2006

British Library Cataloguing in Publication Data
A catalogue record for this book is available from the
British Library
ISBN-10: 1 85437 253 X
ISBN-13: 9 781854 372536

Cover designed by Slatter-Anderson, London
Book designed by Isambard Thomas
Printed in Hong Kong by South Sea International
Press Ltd

Cover: Giacomo Balla, *Abstract Speed: The Car Has Passed*,
1913 (detail of fig.29)

Frontispiece: Umberto Boccioni, *A Futurist Evening in
Milan*, 1911 (detail of fig.23)

Measurements are given in centimetres, height before
width, followed by inches in brackets

Also available in this series:

Abstract Art Mel Gooding
Abstract Expressionism Debra Bricker Balken
Arte Povera Robert Lumley
Conceptual Art Paul Wood
Cubism David Cottington
Expressionism Shulamith Behr
Minimalism David Batchelor
Modernism Charles Harrison
Pop Art David McCarthy
Post-Impressionism Belinda Thomson
Postmodernism Eleanor Heartney
Realism James Malpas
Surrealism Fiona Bradley

General Editor: Simon Wilson

Contents

I

CRASH:
TIME, SEX MACHINES AND THE FOUNDING MANIFESTO

In sul passo dell'Arno	In the crossing of the Arno
I tedeschi hanno lasciato	The Germans have left
Il ricordo della loro civiltà	A souvenir of their good manners

These words were chalked by an Italian on the base of a statue of Dante in the colonnade of the Uffizi, Florence, in August 1944. Referring to the widespread destruction of Italian art and architecture as the Germans retreated in the face of the allied advance northwards, they comment on the finale to an era in Italian history of which Futurism was a noisy and enthusiastic harbinger. Although much was saved from what Churchill called the 'red-hot rake' of the battle line, the disastrous consequences of Italy's alliance with Germany and the end of Benito Mussolini's Fascist regime, were indisputable and irrevocable. The anonymous graffiti forms an ironic epitaph to the visionary bravado and rhetoric of the poet Filippo Tommaso Marinetti (1876–1944) in his 'Founding Manifesto of Futurism' published on the front page of the leading Parisian conservative newspaper *Le Figaro* thirty-five years earlier (fig.1): 'So let them come, the gay incendiaries with charred fingers! Here they are! Here they are! ... Come on! Set fire to the library shelves! Turn aside the canals to flood the museums! ... Oh, the joy of seeing the glorious old canvases bobbing adrift on those waters, discoloured and shredded! ... Take up your pickaxes, your axes and hammers and wreck, wreck the venerable cities, pitilessly!'

'Futurism' is a term that may suggest a number of things. For example, when we describe something as being 'futuristic', we mean to convey an idea of scientific and technological advance beyond that which presently exists. The images and themes of classic science fiction are usually 'futuristic', featuring vast, gleaming, streamlined spacecraft travelling faster than the speed of light to planets billions of miles away. The future is a place in which aliens with unimaginably enormous brains live in cities of mile-high skyscrapers and

1

Front page of *Le Figaro*
20 February 1909,
with the Futurist
manifesto

where personal travel is undertaken by molecular decomposition and reconstitution in booths conveniently placed like ubiquitous bus stops wherever one may wish to go. This notion of the 'futuristic' carries with it not only extraordinary technological development but also a complementary vision of the mind and body transformed, giving human beings new mental and physical powers. In this world we will all be supermen and superwomen, or

perhaps just genderless super-beings. Thus 'futuristic' tends to imply the infinite possibilities of progress for which there are always signs in the present – the futuristic car designs, presented to us today in increasingly sophisticated adverts, conjure up this world that is yet to come. Strangely, it is also a world that may have had its day, suggesting a heroic and naive aspiration typical of the culture of early and mid twentieth-century Europe and America, rather than our darker, less optimistic sense of what lies in store and our forebodings about, for instance, what the writer J.G. Ballard has called 'a nightmare marriage between sex and technology'.

Obviously, 'futurism' also suggests simply an idea of a segment of time, deriving from the structuring of our experience and language around a tripartite scheme of past, present and future. Nineteenth- and twentieth-century philosophers, writers and artists, from the Pre-Raphaelites and Marcel Proust, through Henri Bergson and Umberto Boccioni, to Jean-Paul Sartre and Francis Bacon have been greatly preoccupied with time.

Although modern history cannot claim any monopoly on a concern with the temporal, it is probably true that, in a secular culture where it is thought that God may not be available to underwrite our existence and therefore provide a neat conclusion to human affairs, time has been at a premium for the intellectual classes as they have searched its mysterious store of past and present for clues about the future. Prophecy is one of the skills we often expect from our thinkers and creators and it was certainly something Marinetti and the Futurists believed they possessed in impressive quantities.

The English word 'future', loaded as it is, has its etymological root in the Latin *futurus*, which is the future participle of *esse* (to be). Its origin as a verb therefore places emphasis on the idea of 'that which is to be hereafter'. Although in the science fiction sense of the future as a place there is unavoidably a reference to the verb, it does not carry such a strong sense of the existential meaning of the word and thus of its rootedness in the experience of the 'present in motion'.

These are abstract questions but it is helpful to emphasise the complexity of the terms 'future' and 'futurism' and to clarify the distinction between the idea of the future as a noun and, more or less, a place, on the one hand and, on the other, as a verb and deriving its force from present experience. The Italian Futurists were concerned with these distinct but related meanings and in ways that may at first seem a little surprising. For all their manifesto rhetoric about the city, aeroplanes, telephones and all the other trappings of 'modern life', they rarely painted or described the future itself, in the way, for example, that H.G. Wells did. This is not to say that their art is never about such things, nor that they were unenthusiastic about how technological life might turn out – after all, the great Futurist architect Antonio Sant'Elia drew distinctly futuristic and fantastic cities (fig.2) – but a close look at their art and writing suggests that 'futurism' also meant something else to them. Indeed, their critics frequently pointed out that horses, dogs and scenes of ordinary street life were more prevalent in their paintings than the high-tech images that their pronouncements might lead one to expect. What their leader Marinetti and many of his associates meant by 'Futurism' was as much a rejection of the past

2
Antonio Sant'Elia

*Airport and Railway
Station with Elevators
and Funiculars over
Three-levelled Street*
1914

Ink and pencil on paper
50 x 39 (19¾ × 15¼)
Musei Civici, Como

as an idolatrous concern with the portents of the future. For them, Futurism was a highly politicised philosophy of life rooted in their rejection of a host of forces, which they believed were inimical to the growth and modernisation of Italy. The insistence on the destruction of Italy's heritage is part of this rejection. Violent action, whether in life or art, was seen as the antidote to political, cultural and psychological lethargy. The stultifying feeling that *Bell'Italia* was an albatross around the neck of a new and youthful desire for change was overwhelming, and thus reckless, sublimated sexual behaviour was proposed as the true source of freedom and energy:

> 'Let's go!' I said. 'Friends, away! Let's go! Mythology and the Mystic Ideal are defeated at last. We're about to see the Centaur's birth and, soon after, the first

> flight of Angels! . . . We must shake the gates of life, test the bolts and hinges. Let's go! Look there, on the earth, the very first dawn! There's nothing to match the splendour of the sun's red sword, slashing for the first time through our millennial gloom!'
>
> We went to the three snorting beasts, to lay amorous hands on their torrid breasts. I stretched out on my car like a corpse on its bier, but revived at once under the steering wheel, a guillotine blade that threatened my stomach.
>
> The raging broom of madness swept us out of ourselves and drove us through streets as rough and deep as the beds of torrents. Here and there, sick lamplight through window glass taught us to distrust the deceitful mathematics of our perishing eyes.

With its faintly ludicrous *Toad-of-Toad-Hall*-on-drugs tone, this celebrated passage from the Founding Manifesto of Futurism continues until, inevitably, Marinetti's car crashes into a 'maternal ditch, almost full of muddy water! Fair factory drain! I gulped down your nourishing sludge; and I remembered the blessed black breast of my Sudanese nurse'. A crowd of gawping local fishermen hastily erect a derrick and fish the car out of the ditch thinking it is beyond repair, but Marinetti caresses his 'beautiful shark' and it roars back to life.

David Cronenberg's controversial 1997 film *Crash* (fig.4), based on J.G. Ballard's novel written in 1973, shows a world of perverted desire whose characters, inverting the stereotypes of contemporary car commercials, derive a sick gratification from watching and being involved in motorway crashes. Pleasure and pain mix in a world of remorseless traffic and empty sexual craving. In Marinetti's manifesto, almost ninety years earlier, though sexuality and technology are similarly conjoined in the car crash, the sense of danger is greater than the actual catastrophe and, more significantly, it leads to the full release of tension and to a new creative energy and determination: 'And so, faces smeared with good factory muck, plastered with metallic waste, with senseless sweat, with celestial soot – we, bruised, our arms in slings, but unafraid, declared our high intentions to all the *living* of the earth.' The famous eleven-point manifesto then follows:

1. We intend to sing the love of danger, the habit of energy and fearlessness.
2. Courage, audacity, and revolt will be essential elements of our poetry.
3. Up to now literature has exalted a pensive immobility, ecstasy, and sleep. We intend to exalt aggressive action, a feverish insomnia, the racer's stride, the mortal leap, the punch and the slap.
4. We affirm that the world's magnificence has been enriched by a new beauty: the beauty of speed. A racing car whose hood is adorned with great pipes, like serpents of explosive breath – a roaring car that seems to ride on grapeshot is more beautiful than the *Victory of Samothrace*.
5. We want to hymn the man at the wheel, who hurls the lance of his spirit across the Earth, along the circle of its orbit.
6. The poet must spend himself with ardour, splendour and generosity, to swell the enthusiastic fervour of the primordial elements.
7. Except in struggle, there is no more beauty. No work without an aggressive character can be a masterpiece. Poetry must be conceived as a violent attack on unknown forces, to reduce and prostrate them before man.
8. We stand on the last promontory of the centuries! . . . Why should we look back, when what we want is to break down the mysterious doors of the Impossible? Time and Space died yesterday. We already live in the absolute, because we have created eternal, omnipresent speed.
9. We will glorify war – the world's only hygiene – militarism, patriotism, the destructive gesture of freedom-bringers, beautiful ideas worth dying for, and scorn for woman.
10. We will destroy the museums, libraries, academies of every kind, will fight moralism, feminism, every opportunistic or utilitarian cowardice.
11. We will sing of great crowds excited by work, by pleasure, and by riot; we will sing of the multicoloured, polyphonic tides of revolution in the modern capitals; we will sing of the vibrant nightly fervour of arsenals and shipyards blazing with violent electric moons; greedy clouds by the crooked lines of their smoke; bridges that stride the rivers like giant gymnasts, flashing in the sun with a glitter of knives; adventurous steamers that sniff the horizon; deep-chested locomotives whose wheels paw the tracks like the hooves of enormous steel horses bridled by tubing; and the sleek flight of planes whose propellers chatter in the wind like banners and seem to cheer like an enthusiastic crowd.

That the outcome of Marinetti's crazy, phallic drive through the night in his sex machine should be expressed in the classic political form of a manifesto, as well as in the announcement of a new, at this stage literary, movement is important to note. Although in a sense Marinetti is driving his libido towards a brave new world of the future, anticipating the notion that the car is a symbol of personal freedom, the key motive is the race from the atavistic pull of the past and the engagement of present desire with present reality. Spaceships might or might not follow.

3

F.T. Marinetti in his automobile 1908

4

Still from *Crash* (1997), directed by David Cronenberg

2

THE CONDITIONS FOR FUTURISM

5

Aerial view of the
Vittorio Emmanuele II
monument, Rome

In 1909 Italy was still a very young nation and one ill at ease with its past as well
as its present and anticipated future. The country's economy was growing
rapidly, and a powerful, if precarious, sense of nationhood had developed.
Futurism was an intrinsic part of this volatile context, and its strengths and
weaknesses as a movement derive in large part from the national circumstances
in which it evolved. It was also self-consciously international in its ambitions:
its relations with the avant-garde culture of other parts of Europe, as well as its
response to the host of scientific and technological changes that were
dramatically altering people's experience across the world, are key factors for an
understanding of its particular character. This chapter will give a brief account
of some of the most important elements forming the background to Futurism.

In 1861, after forty years of political struggle, the fragile new state of Italy
was proclaimed. This often violent progress towards nationhood had been part
of a wider European development, which saw, in Germany for example, new
political structures and cultural identities forming under the pressures of
unavoidable economic, technological and social change. In Italy unification was
not immediate and absolute. The new king Vittorio Emmanuele III and his
government were based in Turin and Piedmont, and their powerful elite in the
north dominated the new country. The extraordinary Vittorio Emmanuele II
monument, built provocatively at the heart of the ancient papal state of Rome
as the 'altar of the nation' and known to many Romans as 'The False Teeth', was
a grandiose, almost burlesque statement of this new power (fig.5). Its

gargantuan marble pretensions express many of the contradictory forces at work in modern Italy, which the Futurists would later seek to harness. The financial circumstances of the country overall were almost continuously parlous and the heavy taxes necessary to balance the national budget created enormous discontent, especially in the poorer areas of the south. While the great industrial cities of Milan, Turin and Genoa expanded enormously under a liberal regime, other areas remained economically disadvantaged and the strains of this imbalance between the regions led to a dangerous fragmentation at the political level. By the 1880s, its problems exacerbated by a global depression, Italy was facing widespread poverty and the ensuing disillusion and discontent led to the formation of many political groups in urban and rural areas prepared to take violent action to fight their cause in the absence of a wider franchise. The artist Pelizza da Volpedo, an important precursor of the Futurists, portrayed the organised power of the masses in his huge canvas *The Fourth Estate* (fig.6). By the 1890s, government measures expanding the electorate, protecting domestic economies, providing subsidies and increasing investment

led to a marked improvement in the economy, although the action taken still favoured the industrial north and left the agrarian south in a state of near crisis.

In the sphere of international policy the government began a period of colonial expansion in Africa, hoping to achieve a nationalist consensus and to extend markets for the growing home economy. Although both aspirations were severely limited by the sheer range and power of the imperial interests of Britain, France and Germany, it was of utmost importance for Italians to demonstrate on a world stage that they were part of the 'aristocracy' of European nations. Such attitudes were later to become part and parcel of Futurist propaganda as it sought to take a specifically Italian variety of modernism to the rest of the continent and beyond.

The authoritarian administration of Francesco Crispi in the late 1880s and early 1890s created corruption at the highest levels of government and society as well as the suppression of the new reformist Socialist Party. When Italy was defeated by the Abyssinians at the Battle of Adua in 1896, however, Crispi's days were numbered and Giovanni Giolitti came to power. Giolitti pursued moderate policies, which were designed to ensure greater stability and steady economic growth and were underpinned by a move to greater consensus among different classes and interest groups. He further extended the franchise, although he always operated with a minority, and introduced a wide range of legislation intended to ameliorate social and political inequalities and conflict. The fact that he was the figurehead of Italy's *belle époque* made him vulnerable to charges of decadence and corruption by his radical enemies.

Giolitti's problem was the continued prevalence, in spite of his reforms, of small but determined marginal groups of anarchists, syndicalists, nationalists and extreme socialists who disapproved of his pragmatic compromises and lack of radical vision. From many of these groups there emerged a broad though disunited movement demanding a nationalistic, expansionist, corporate state. War and social integration were seen by those supporting this tendency as two of the crucial impetuses for national rejuvenation. Young intellectuals and artists, attracted by this dynamic ideology, became fierce opponents of Giolitti and sought political ideas and cultural forms with which to express their impatience and frustration. Marinetti, who preferred the colonialism of Crispi, was no doubt one of those discontented readers of the magazine *La Voce* who would have enthusiastically agreed with the writer Giovanni Amendola's critique of *Giolittismo* in 1910, when he wrote: 'Disgust and pity fills us when we look back over the past decades of political and administrative life in our

kingdom and see how they have been irremediably stamped by the moral deficiency and intellectual poverty of our ruling class. With impatience and anger do we take stock of the enormous obstacles which we have to remove from the path that will lead our people towards a national life in tune with our present ideals and needs.' This sense of betrayal should not be underestimated and it explains the strength of the vision held by many intellectuals that a profound reorganisation of Italian society based on entirely new philosophical premises was urgently required. The violence of the language indicates the strength of feeling that, as we have already seen, was to become a hallmark of Futurist rhetoric. Typical of the literature of this political culture, for example, was the journal *La Demolizione*, edited by Ottavio Dinale, dedicated to 'vast social battle' and publisher of Marinetti's Futurist manifesto. Giolitti, his parliament, government and supporters among the industrialists and landowners, so Dinale believed, would be crushed in the same way that Italy's stifling and humiliating cultural dependency on its 'dead' museum culture would be demolished to make way for the new art of the future. The struggle to define the nature of this new art was at the heart of the Futurist project. When Mussolini's Fascist state seized power following the 'March on Rome' in 1922, the embodiment so it seemed of these earlier expressions of political and cultural renewal, it also inherited all the uncertainties and contradictions in the artistic and cultural sphere, which, as ever, remained unresolved. Futurism and Fascism were indissolubly linked, as we shall see, but in a subtly strained, puzzling and even comic relationship. Mussolini promoted certain aspects of Futurism while remaining extremely wary of, and even openly hostile to, others.

This turbulent political background specific to Italy should also be considered against a wider set of conditions that were affecting all Europeans, and indeed the inhabitants of many other countries, in less definite but nevertheless real ways in the years around the turn of the twentieth century. The writer Stephen Kern has described 'a series of sweeping changes in technology and culture [that] created distinctive new modes of thinking about and experiencing time and space. Technological innovations including the telephone, wireless telegraph, x-ray, cinema, bicycle, automobile, and airplane established the material foundation for this reorientation; independent cultural developments such as the stream-of-consciousness novel, psychoanalysis, Cubism, and the theory of relativity shaped consciousness directly. The result was a transformation of the dimensions of life and thought.' The Futurists in particular were keen to 'shape consciousness directly' in the light of such changes. Their vision of a new Italy was grounded in the material and cognitive experience shared to a greater or lesser extent by all their fellow countrymen. They were certainly not alone in observing the significance of these new conditions, but they approached them with an aesthetic and intellectual purpose that was unique in its focus and technical means.

Many of these aspects of the early Futurist culture are best discovered and examined through the artworks and writings of the figures we shall be discussing in subsequent chapters. However, there are certain areas that require a degree of amplification at this stage because they lie at the core of the general consciousness of the international audience to which the Futurists directed their practices.

Firstly, the changes in the means and speed of communication had profound effects. Aside from steam-powered ships and trains, motorcars and, most recently, aeroplanes, one of the most important changes arrived with the development of wireless telegraphy. In 1894 the Italian Guglielmo Marconi, naturally a Futurist hero, invented an apparatus that transmitted electromagnetic waves and by 1904 his new company had established the first transatlantic wireless news company. The possibilities afforded by such technology suggested a new network of invisible waves criss-crossing the world and breaking down the slow, unilinear time of the past. With the concurrent growth of telephone usage there was a novel awareness of the world as a dynamic interaction of simultaneous events, often thousands of miles apart, but which could be experienced in an instant. The social ramifications of such developments were not lost on contemporary commentators, many of whom anticipated the 'global village' described by the Canadian cultural theorist

6
Giuseppe Pelizza da Volpedo

The Fourth Estate
1898–1901

Oil on canvas
283 x 550 (111 x 216)
Civica Galleria d'Arte
Moderna, Milan

Marshall McLuhan many years later. With photography and cinema developing during this period there was a new experience of the instantaneous and the simultaneous, which gripped many artists and writers, from James Joyce, who was instrumental in opening the first cinema in Dublin in 1909 and whose literary techniques reflected the new sense of time, to Cubist painters such as Pablo Picasso in his fragmentary canvases, and Sonia Delaunay, who illustrated Blaise Cendrars's poem *Prose on the Trans-Siberian Railway and of Little Jehanne of France* in 1913 (fig.7). This work, a two metre 'scroll', describes a train journey from Moscow to Harbin, and includes a map and an abstract evocation of the journey by Delaunay which, along with Cendrars' words, evoke a Whitmanesque world of speed, disrupted time and mechanical personal experience:

> Now I've made all the trains run after me
> Basel–Timbuktu
> I've also played the horses at Auteuil and at Longchamps
> Paris–New York
> Now I've made all the trains run alongside my life
> Madrid–Stockholm.

The railway station of a Victorian painter such as William Powell Frith had changed from being a place of arrival and departure to a point on a kaleidoscopic mental map of desire. Like the French poet and critic Guillaume Apollinaire, some of whose poetry investigated through broken syntax and rhythms the sexual fantasies embedded in the new consciousness, Marinetti and the Futurists brought to their work a sense of the libidinal energy that seemed to be driving the intricate technological and psychological changes.

Although Futurism is often equated simply with 'machismo' there were in fact a number of female Futurists, and one of them, Valentine de Saint-Point, the French poet, dancer and exponent of the need for a Nietzschean 'superwoman', wrote a 'Futurist Manifesto of Lust' in 1913, which succinctly defined the relationship between sexuality and modernity: 'LUST EXCITES ENERGY AND RELEASES STRENGTH. Pitilessly it drove primitive man to victory, for the pride of bearing back to a woman the spoils of the defeated. Today it drives the great men of business who direct the banks, the press and international trade to increase their wealth by creating centres, harnessing energies and exalting the crowds, to

7

Sonia Delaunay

Prose on the Trans-Siberian Railway and of Little Jehanne of France
1913

Paper 195.6 × 35.6
(77 × 14)
Tate Gallery

8

Luigi Russolo

Nietzsche and Madness
1907–8

Etching
Civica Raccolta delle Stampe Achille Bertarelli, Castell Sforzesco, Milan

worship and glorify with it the object of their lust.' Machines, the 'life-force', capitalism and a violent sexual impulse were inextricably linked in the Futurist imagination with historical forces against which they believed it was futile to struggle.

The Futurists were mainly artists and writers and thus their interest was to present this wholly unprecedented range of new experiences in their work, focused by a sense of their historical mission as the avant-garde of a rejuvenated Italy. They were unusually promiscuous in their pursuit of ideas and images and happily plundered the efforts of many others as they gathered the elements of Futurist art into a coherent and distinct synthesis. There were, however, two thinkers whose ideas were particularly significant in the formation of Futurism and, indeed, in the development of early modernism as a whole: Friedrich Nietzsche (1844–1900) and Henri Bergson (1859–1941).

Nietzsche, celebrated for having announced in 1882 the 'death of god', has suffered from selective misinterpretation by detractors and disciples alike. The Futurists were disciples and duly misread Nietzsche for their own particular purposes (fig.8). Nietzsche's philosophy, written in a hybrid, aphoristic style in works such as *Thus Spoke Zarathustra* (1883–5) and *The Will to Power* (1887), attempted to break through the fragmented rationalism of modern culture and morality, to go 'beyond good and evil'. His rejection of Christianity and return to the culture of classical Greece demanded that the modern individual create his own system of values. In *The Birth of Tragedy* (1872) he contrasted the 'Apollonian' spirit, which is based on order and reason, with the 'Dionysian' – that which draws on the deep and chaotic forces of life and in which modern man should immerse himself. From this supreme 'will to power' would emerge the 'superman', the man who transcends the limitations and mediocrity of the contemporary world and who rises above the crowd. Ultimately, this individual would be the heroic artist: 'only as an aesthetic phenomenon is the world and the existence of man eternally justified.' Art, in Nietzsche's version of things, is the product of a restless, tragic, Dionysian soul that constantly recreates the world in aesthetic form and in doing so destroys the deadening accretions of the past. The artist spins an endless web of illusory form, which eventually becomes the habit of others. He is a kind of displaced leader in a god-less world radically disorientated by modernity: 'What were we doing when we unchained this earth from its sun? Whither is it moving now? Whither are we moving? Away from all suns? Are we not plunging continually?

Backward, sideward, forward, in all directions? Is there still any up or down? Are we not straying as through an infinite nothing? Do we not feel the breath of empty space?' The Futurists, among many others, sought to (mis)interpret Nietzsche's vision and to realise in themselves the concept of the superman. Similar ambitions led to more catastrophic outcomes in the cases of Hitler and Mussolini.

Whereas Nietzsche concerned himself with the idea of new values, the French philosopher Henri Bergson reconceived ideas of time and 'becoming'. In his important early book *An Introduction to Metaphysics*, published in 1893, he described time as a flux through which human consciousness flows and evolves even while the individual personality retains in this process its unique selfhood. Bergson, at pains to stress the difficulty of expressing his ideas, called human experience through time 'duration'. He distinguished between two modes of knowledge: the 'relative', which seeks to know something by external observation and analysis, and the 'absolute', which, by 'intuition', is achieved through a kind of intellectual sympathy with the inward reality of an object.

Thus, for Bergson, mechanical clock time was antithetical to 'duration' and the clock itself the rigid symbol of a kind of death-in-life. Hailing the intuitive faculties of the artist (and, incidentally, the insect) and the potential of new forms of art to flow with dynamic flux, where we 'will see the material world melt back into a single flux, a continuity of flowing, a becoming', Bergson, ironically, took a poor view of the many avant-garde artists among his army of admirers who sought to produce art out of theory.

Bergson's lectures at the Collège de France in Paris and on extensive European tours before the First World War were enormously popular with a wide-ranging audience (fig.9), which included artists such as Wyndham Lewis, writers like Marinetti and Apollinaire, and the influential syndicalist political theorist Georges Sorel, as well as an enthusiastic general public. Bergson's most successful and widely read book was *Creative Evolution* published in 1907. Following the ideals of Charles Darwin, it characterised evolution in terms of a life-force that, like an exploding shell shot from a gun, continues to fragment and to create different life forms from plants to human beings. He believed that this dynamic process could slow down and that the machine was startling evidence of this tendency. As we shall see, Bergson saw laughter as the vital internal response of man to this danger of mechanisation. His complex ideas were interpreted in many contradictory ways by a diverse audience, but he set forth a constellation of themes and a richly suggestive vocabulary that dominate the intellectual discourse of the period before 1914. Duration, intuition, evolution, the life-force, habit – all these terms occur throughout the dense web of discussions between artists, writers and theorists and affected all levels of thought and creativity in Europe.

THE PAINTERS: FIRST RESPONSES

'If our pictures are Futurist, it is because they are the result of absolutely Futurist conceptions, ethical, aesthetic, political, social', claimed the Futurists in the catalogue for an exhibition held in London in 1912. Marinetti's call for a new art was met by a number of Italian painters who responded to the vague but stirring language of the manifesto. We have seen that such language was not produced in a vacuum but was part of a disparate radical agenda for political and cultural change shared by the avant-garde intellectuals of the period. Giacomo Balla (1871–1958), Umberto Boccioni (1882–1916) and Carlo Carrà (1881–1966), among others who signed the 'Manifesto of the Futurist Painters' in 1910, were already inclined to an interest in the heated, *fin-de-siècle* fantasy mixed with modernist machine-worship and extremist political rhetoric of Marinetti's manifesto. Each of them had developed practices as painters in response to the complex options available to them at the end of the century – Social Realism, Symbolism, Impressionism and neo-Impressionism being just a few of the international styles within which their art had been formed. Most of these technical movements had broader values and political beliefs attached to them. One of the most important of these was a Nietzschean conviction that the artist and his work had a significance beyond the studio, salon or museum and that the artist's vision was at a critical 'cutting edge' that set the pace for society's development. Thus the 'avant-garde', by definition, was ahead of the rest of mankind, the latter, as it were, catching up, reluctantly but inevitably, with the pioneering vision.

Balla's pre-Futurist painting reveals an artist with a strong commitment to socialist politics and to the depiction of the working class, the dispossessed and the marginalised in society, such as bankrupts and the insane. In *A Worker's Day*, painted in 1904 (fig.10), he divides the canvas into three to show, in a manner indebted to Claude Monet's famous series of Impressionist paintings of the same subject in changing light, three moments during the working day of some building labourers. The frame is painted to look like brickwork, which both illustrates the nature of his subjects' work and emphasises the theme of construction – a theme, along with the depiction of change through time, that features prominently in Futurist art. While there is some reference to traditional images of the cycle of work, seen here under evolving light conditions, there is a strong, if melancholy, sense of modernity in the geometrical formation of the building under construction and the impression of human life ordered by the determining physical and psychological grid of urban life.

Street Light (fig.11), probably painted by Balla in 1909 (though the dating is uncertain), was inspired by one of the first electric street lamps to be installed in Rome where he was based, and was probably an initial response to

Marinetti's manifesto and other contemporary writing. It deliberately juxtaposes the rays violently discharged in multi-coloured darts by the street light with a rather feeble crescent moon that seems to be circling it. Balla may have been inspired in this modest, but crudely effective painting by Marinetti's early Futurist prose piece 'Let's Murder the Moonlight' of April 1909, in which he described a typically fantastic midnight escapade:

> A cry went up in the airy solitude of the high plains: 'Let's Murder the moonlight!' Some ran to nearby cascades; gigantic wheels were raised, and turbines transformed the rushing waters into magnetic pulses that rushed up wires, up high poles, up to shining, humming globes.
>
> So it was that three hundred electric moons cancelled with their rays of blinding mineral whiteness the ancient green queen of loves.

Here, the contemporary electrification of Italy evokes a man-made or masculine light source that overcomes the feminine power of the moon, the mythical source of the sea's rhythm, love and madness. The hidden theme of 'scorn for woman' is significant. For Marinetti and many of the Futurists, 'Woman' was 'anti-modern' and resisted change. However, this apparently misogynist tendency should be seen against a broader Futurist ambition to create 'a non-human type'. As the literary critic Peter Nicholls has pointed out: 'Although Marinetti's fantasy of a new heroic existence amounted to a dream of super-masculinity, it thrived on the "paradox" that the lack and inadequacy which it aimed to abolish were the entailments not merely of traditional

10
Giacomo Balla

A Worker's Day 1904

Oil on card 100 × 135
(39½ × 53)
Private Collection

11
Giacomo Balla

Street Light 1909

Oil on canvas
174.7 × 114.5
(68¾ × 45¼)
The Museum of Modern
Art, New York. Hillman
Periodicals Fund

femininity but of sexual difference itself.' Marinetti had written in 1909 in the magazine *Poesia* of 'the terrible nausea we get from the obsession with the ideal woman in works of the imagination, the tyranny of love amongst Latin people'. Thus we can see how Balla's painting carries a weight of complex, even contradictory, cultural concerns beyond questions of technique or stylistic appropriation.

Umberto Boccioni, who was Balla's student in Rome at the turn of the century, shared the older artist's socialist and humanitarian vision and the concomitant idea that humans are the product of their environment. He was also a devotee of Nietzsche, whose writings, as we have seen, were crucial to Futurist thinking. In Balla's studio Boccioni learned the principles of Divisionism, the Italian version of French neo-Impressionism, in which small dots, patches and lines of pigment are organised with quasi-scientific precision to emulate natural light and atmosphere.

After a period travelling in Europe, Boccioni returned to Italy and finally settled in Milan in 1907. He had begun to renounce what he saw as the

12
Umberto Boccioni

Factories at Porta Romana 1909

Oil on canvas
75 × 145
(29½ × 57)
Banca Commerciale Italiana, Milan

13
Carlo Carrà

Leaving the Theatre 1910–11

Oil on canvas
69 × 91
(27 × 35¾)
Estorick Foundation, London

limitations of Balla's realist aesthetic and, under the influence of the painter and colour theorist Gaetano Previati, turned to a personal version of Symbolism, which was also indebted to the art of the Norwegian artist Edvard Munch. By 1909, however, Boccioni had identified his art with more obviously modern interests in his subject matter and technique. Indeed as early as 1907, anticipating the spirit of the first Futurist manifesto, he had written in his diary that, 'I feel I want to paint what is new, the product of our industrial time. I am nauseated by old walls, old palaces, old subjects based on reminiscences: I want to have my eye on the life of our day'. His *Factories at Porta Romana* 1909 (fig.12) shows an industrial area on the northern edge of Milan where he lived, and continues the theme of contemporary construction and urban expansion found in Balla's *A Worker's Day* of five years earlier. Developing the Divisionist technique he had learned under Balla and Previati, Boccioni suggests the vibrant energy of agricultural land as it undergoes transformation into a suburb of factories with new roads, workers' tenements and chimneys belching smoke. It is uncertain whether this work was painted before or after the publication of Marinetti's founding manifesto, but it is clearly engaged with the heroic industrialisation seen by contemporary radicals as a symbol of the modernisation of Italy.

Carlo Carrà who, like Boccioni, was based in Milan, had also developed during the opening few years of the century a Divisionist technique allied to a realist subject matter that he had inherited from his teacher at the Accademia di Brera in Milan, Cesare Tallone. In works such as *Leaving the Theatre* (fig.13) Carrà presents a nocturnal metropolitan world irradiated by electric light in which the spectral human figures seem to melt into a multi-coloured atmosphere where foreground and background are merged across the picture plane. The

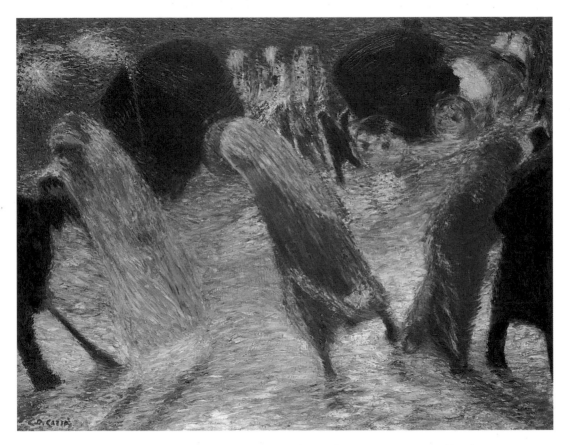

sense of anti-climax at the end of a performance is conveyed by the stooping figures as they dissolve into the night. As in much of the Futurist painting that was to follow shortly after such works as this, there is a strong tendency to subordinate the human being to the forces of the environment and to suggest a blurring of the boundaries between separate individuals and the inanimate forms surrounding them. Psychological and physical space are merged.

The signatories of the 'Manifesto of the Futurist Painters', published in a leaflet on 11 February 1910, repeated the typical Marinettian bombast about hatred of the past, the 'triumphant progress of science' and the rebirth of Italy. Artists are urged to engage their work with the modern world and to 'breathe in the tangible miracles of contemporary life – the iron network of speedy communications which envelops the earth, the transatlantic liners, the dreadnoughts, those marvellous flights which follow our skies, the profound courage of our submarine navigators and the spasmodic struggle to conquer the unknown. How can we remain insensible to the frenetic life of our great cities and to the exciting new psychology of night-life … ?' The final key points of the manifesto convey a general exhortation to 'elevate all attempts at originality, however daring, however violent', without telling us much more that is helpful in identifying what the new art would actually look like.

The same painters' 'Futurist Painting: Technical Manifesto', launched at a riotous event at the Chiarella Theatre in Turin on 18 March of the same year, gives a far stronger sense of the aesthetic direction the movement would initially take as it sought to create an art in tune with Marinetti's vision. The key points are as follows:

> The gesture which we would reproduce on canvas shall no longer be a fixed *moment* in universal dynamism. It shall simply be the *dynamic sensation* itself.
>
> Indeed, all things move, all things run, all things are rapidly changing. A profile is never motionless before our eyes, but it constantly appears and disappears. On account of the persistency of an image upon the retina moving objects constantly multiply themselves; their form changes like rapid vibrations, in their mad career. Thus a running horse has not four legs, but twenty, and their movements are triangular …
>
> To paint a human figure you must not paint it; you must render the whole of its surrounding atmosphere …
>
> Who can still believe in the opacity of bodies, since our sharpened and multiplied sensitiveness has already penetrated the obscure manifestations of the medium? …
>
> Painters have shown us the objects and people placed before us. We shall henceforward put the spectator in the centre of the picture.

Thus the central point is that the modern world experienced by the city dwellers of the new twentieth century is one of movement, dynamism, transparency and radiant coloured light. The consciousness of man in this world is a restless and multi-dimensional one that 'does not permit us to look upon man as the centre of universal life. The suffering of a man is of the same interest to us as the suffering of an electric lamp, which, with spasmodic starts, shrieks out the most heartrending expressions of colour'. Man and his environment are in a constantly dynamic relationship in which 'movement and light destroy the materiality of bodies', and the medium by which this relationship will be expressed is the colour of Divisionism, 'which must be an innate complementariness which we declare to be essential and necessary'. The new Futurist painters therefore used their commitment to the chromatic fundamentals of Impressionism as the basis of an art responsive to the broad principles of Marinetti's modernist vision. They soon realised, however, that this would not be enough to deliver an art that truly reflected their complex aesthetic and psychological aspirations.

Between 1909 and 1911, therefore, we find the Futurist painters moving rapidly through a series of technical changes, which opened up for them new opportunities to create a truly radical art. Increasingly, of course, their subject matter reflected the fascination with the characteristics of modernity expressed in their manifestos: riots, industrial labour, trams, night scenes and so on. Their colour is applied in ever brighter and more strident combinations, in keeping with their declaration that 'yellow shines forth in our flesh, that red blazes, and that green, blue and violet dance upon it with untold charms, voluptuous and caressing'.

A work such as Boccioni's large painting *The City Rises*, begun in August or September 1910 (fig.14), represents this first stage of experimentation at its height of energy and ambition. Boccioni described it the same year in a letter to his friend the critic Nino Barbantini as 'a great synthesis of labour, light and movement', going on prophetically to say that it 'may well be a work of transition, and I believe one of the last'. Hoping to create a picture that

conveyed emotion through form and colour rather than mere description, Boccioni wrote to his lover Ines that, 'Now I understand the fever, passion, love, violence meant when one says to oneself: Create! . . . How I understand Marinetti's dictum: No work that lacks an aggressive character can be a masterwork'. Here are the sentiments of a true devotee of Marinetti and perhaps they also suggest a weakness in Boccioni's position. When the work was exhibited at the Arte Libera exhibition in Milan in May 1911, Barbantini wrote in an article that 'by and large it is not in accord with Boccioni's character to persist in symbolic painting'. Boccioni was wounded by this critique and replied that he had been inspired by the need to erect 'a new altar of modern life vibrant with dynamism . . . no less pure and exalting than those raised out of religious contemplation of the divine mystery'. It is certainly the case that

Boccioni painted an image of violently energetic action in a building site with labourers restraining a huge horse in the foreground while, behind them, buildings surrounded by scaffolding are being constructed and crowds and trams move through an urban landscape of chimneys and telegraph poles. The complementary colours, the dissolution of physical bodies and the attempt to force the spectator in to the 'centre' of the painting's action are all present. The sense of dynamism is enhanced by the transformation of the horse's collar into a blue vortex or propeller blade in motion. In spite of these features and the scale of the work, however, there is truth in the contention of many critics in relation to this painting, which, over the next couple of years, was exhibited across Europe and which became a 'classic' Futurist work in the public's mind, that it is a grandiose and heroic gesture rooted in late nineteenth-century Symbolism and not the herald of the brand new art form that was so clearly required by the language of the Futurists' manifestos. It was the impact of the Cubist painting of Picasso, Georges Braque and other artists based in Paris that was the decisive factor in transforming the practice of Boccioni and his colleagues during the course of 1910 and 1911. By 1912, Futurist painting had forged a new vocabulary and was able to make a serious claim to be amongst the most innovative and radical art of its time. This challenge was made known to other artists and to a curious and often hostile public through a series of exhibitions, events, manifestos and publicity stunts orchestrated by Marinetti throughout major European cities in the years leading up to the First World War.

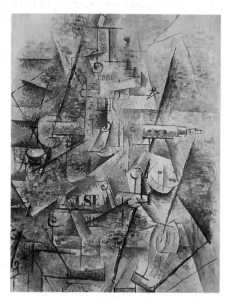

15
Georges Braque
Clarinet and Bottle of Rum on a Mantelpiece
1911

Oil on canvas
81 × 60
(32 × 23¾)
Tate Gallery

16
Gino Severini
Self-Portrait 1912–13

Oil on canvas
55 × 46
(21¾ × 18)
Private Collection

17
Umberto Boccioni
The Laugh 1911

Oil on canvas
110.2 × 145.4
(43½ × 57¼)
The Museum of Modern Art, New York. Gift of Herbert and Nannette Rothschild

Cubism had created a way of painting that completely changed the rules of the visual arts. Concentrating usually on traditional subject matter such as landscape, portraiture and, above all, still life (fig.15), the Cubists analysed form and space in such a way as to break down objects into a matrix of semi-transparent fragments in which surface and depth are no longer distinct. Facets of mute colour and broken lines were deployed to present motifs from a variety of viewpoints until, by 1910 and 1911, when the Futurists first took serious notice of these works, the canvas offered a dense field of ambiguous signs and dappled brushwork. *Trompe-l'oeil* elements such as lettering or illusionistically painted nails were placed at intervals across the picture plane to highlight the play between the real and the artificial, which Picasso and Braque made one of the prime concerns of their new art.

Gino Severini (1883–1966), a signatory of the Futurist painters' opening manifestos, had been working in Paris since 1906, and was one of the main channels between his Italian colleagues and the new developments in the French capital. His *Self-Portrait* of 1912–13 (fig.16) shows how Cubist technique became a vehicle for a new Futurist style. While remaining committed to the

iconography of the modern world, to the concept of a dynamically interactive universe of human movement in a changed technical environment, and to the power of strong and even vulgar colour, the Futurists saw in the luminously static constructions of Cubist art the possibilities of a completely new direction for their work. Above all, it was Cubism's interpenetration of form and space, transparency and multiple viewpoints that the Futurists adapted to their own distinct ideological and imaginative interests. Although sensitive to the criticism of Italian critics such as Ardengo Soffici, who compared their early works unfavourably with those of the Cubists, they set aside nationalistic jealousies and embarked upon a period of intense experimentation. In the

18
Umberto Boccioni

States of Mind I –
The Farewells 1911

Oil on canvas
70.5 × 96.2
(27¾ × 37½)
The Museum of Modern
Art, New York. Gift of
Nelson A. Rockefeller

19
Umberto Boccioni

States of Mind II –
Those Who Go 1911

Oil on canvas
70.8 × 95.9
(28 × 37¾)
The Museum of Modern
Art, New York. Gift of
Nelson A. Rockefeller

process they produced works of great visual power which, they believed, went beyond the limitations of Cubism towards a truly dynamic representation of a world of motion and emotion.

Boccioni, typically, took a deeply theoretical approach to his translation of Cubism into a distinctly Futurist mode. We have seen that the ideas of Bergson were highly influential in avant-garde circles during this period and Boccioni was exemplary in his adaptation of the philosopher's ideas to his interpretation of Cubism. In *The Laugh* of 1911 (fig.17), for example, which is the first of his paintings to show the influence of Cubism, probably after considerable reworking over a more Divisionist first effort, we not only see the artist creating a world of Bergsonian flux, intuition and memory traces, but also a commentary on the Frenchman's theory of laughter. Bergson saw laughter as a kind of organic release of tension in response to the sight of any human who has become rigid or mechanical in their behaviour and thereby ridiculous to behold. At the heart of this theory was a concept of the *élan vital*, or life-force, and its opposite, the ossified forms of dead matter. Boccioni's group of heavily made-up and bejewelled prostitutes sitting around a table in a garishly lit café explode with laughter, perhaps at the expense of the bald, moustached man on the left who seems to be grimacing uncomfortably. Fashionable Thonet chairs, glass-topped tables and large globed lights in an apparently mirrored interior are shown intersecting with the animated figures in a world of brittle egos, nervous laughter and brutal vulgarity.

It was in his *States of Mind* triptych of 1911, however, that Boccioni made his first great statement of Futurist painting, bringing his interests in Bergson, Cubism and the individual's complex experience of the modern world together in what has been described as one of the 'minor masterpieces' of early twentieth-century painting. The work is an attempt to convey feelings and sensations experienced through a passage of time, using the new means of expression described in various writings of the period. These included 'lines of force', which were intended to convey the directional tendencies of objects through space and to draw the spectator's perceptions and emotional responses into the heart of the picture; 'simultaneity', which combined memories, present impressions and anticipation of future events in an orchestrated whole; and 'emotional ambience', in which the artist seeks by intuition the sympathies and links that exist between the exterior (concrete) scene and the interior (abstract) emotion.

In the triptych, the painting subtitled *The Farewells* (fig.18) presents transparent fragments of a locomotive seen from various angles and the flowing forms of embracing figures caught up in waves of smoke, time-flow and pulsing radio signals. True to Futurist doctrine, the colours are not naturalistic but, rather, intended to exaggerate certain subjective emotional states. The image is thus a rhythmically organised hieroglyph suggestive of memory flashes, anguished feelings of separation and the excited anticipation of travel. Vulnerable human bodies and the metallic forms of the locomotive are merged in a synthesis suggestive of a heightened consciousness attempting to hold together the contradictions of the experience of time in an almost superhuman effort of will power. It is important to stress this transcendental

20
Umberto Boccioni

*States of Mind III –
Those Who Stay* 1911

Oil on canvas
70.8 × 95.7
(28 × 37¾)
The Museum of Modern
Art, New York. Gift of
Nelson A. Rockefeller

sense because Boccioni believed in a higher purpose in his art of creating what he called 'spiritualised objective elements' through almost mystical 'pure mathematical values' that would provide the viewer with an equivalent for the artist's state of mind. Such ambitious ideas of a new means of visual communication were shared with many avant-garde artists in Europe during this period. *Those Who Go* (fig.19), dominated by a cold, mechanical blue tone, shows the oblique force lines of the passengers' movement in the train as it speeds past a fragmentary landscape of buildings. In *Those Who Stay* (fig.20), vertical lines form a mournful green veil through which despondent figures disappear. Boccioni wrote of this part

of the work that 'the mathematically spiritualised silhouettes render the distressing melancholy of the soul of those that are left behind'. This is the language of the many late nineteenth-century Symbolist theories that saw colour and form as analogous to music, but which here have been given a Futurist twist. James McNeill Whistler or Paul Gauguin would have understood the ideas, even if no doubt they would have been amazed by the visual result.

Carrà's *The Funeral of the Anarchist Galli* of 1911 (fig.21) is a large canvas commemorating a particular political incident witnessed by the artist in 1904. The celebrated anarchist had been killed during the general strike of that year and at his funeral the police's insistence that the ceremony should take place outside the cemetery provoked a riot. Carrà, who was himself closely involved in anarchist and syndicalist politics, used this by now legendary incident as the source for a contemporary history painting that evokes the violent clash between freedom fighters and the forces of law and order as a visual manifesto of Futurist political and aesthetic convictions. Indeed, he made significant alterations to the painting before exhibiting it, in order to introduce a more Cubist and geometrical edge, thereby accentuating its radical message. While there are clearly references to Italian quattrocento artists such as Paolo Uccello (for Carrà was a keen student of his native Italian painting traditions), such historical references are subordinated to the devices of Futurist painting at a critical stage in its development. The dominant emotional mood of anger and aggression is conveyed through the reds and oranges, while a more ominous tone is present in the anarchist blacks and the deep blues of the figures. Here,

21
Carlo Carrà

The Funeral of the Anarchist Galli 1911

Oil on canvas
198.7 × 259.1
(82¼ × 102)
The Museum of Modern Art, New York. Acquired through the Lillie P. Bliss Bequest

22
Luigi Russolo

Revolt 1911

Oil on canvas
150 × 230m
(59 × 45¼)
Haags Gemeentemuseum, The Hague

the 'force lines' of the technical manifesto are used to draw the spectator into the heart of the action as Carrà attempts to politicise his audience through form and colour.

The painting makes a fascinating comparison with a work by Carrà's associate Luigi Russolo (1885–1947) of the same year (fig.22). *Revolt*, with its diagrammatic red chevrons indicating the waves of revolutionary force thrusting into the city, represents the idea of the unified masses in their struggle for power. In the spirit of the Futurist political manifestos published by Marinetti in 1909 and 1917, Russolo shows 'the collision of two forces, that of the revolutionary element made up of enthusiasm and red lyricism against the force of inertia and reactionary resistance'. Further comparison of Russolo's painting with Pelizza da Volpedo's *The Fourth Estate* (fig.6), painted a decade earlier, offers a telling insight into the extraordinary changes in Italian art over such a short period of time.

Both *Revolt* and *The Funeral of the Anarchist Galli* were shown at the Free Art Exhibition in Milan in 1911, organised by the Casa del Lavoro (House of Labour) as a charity event in aid of the unemployed. Boccioni was part of the organising committee and used the exhibition as an opportunity to promote Futurism and its ideology. In line with Marinetti's libertarian thinking Boccioni not only exhibited Futurist painting but also works by amateurs, children and workers. In a press release for the exhibition he wrote of the 'search for an art that is more ingenious, instinctive, sincere, and which returns to the healthy origins of creativity'. This art 'is not the privilege of a few, but is inborn in human nature' and is typified by 'a universal language of forms and colours ... subconsciously reflected and vividly expressed' in the work of children and proletarians 'struck by their imaginations'. Although most organised socialist groups were highly suspicious of Futurism and indeed all avant-garde art, there is little doubt that many workers in Milan and Turin were drawn to Futurism by such exhibitions. By these means, along with the usually turbulent and even incendiary lectures and Futurist *serata* (evenings) (fig.23) put on by Marinetti and his compatriots in the theatres and halls of the great industrial cities of the north, the group made sure that it was permanently in the news.

23
Umberto Boccioni
A Futurist Evening in Milan 1911
Ink on paper
Whereabouts unknown
On the stage are Boccioni, Balilla Pratella, Marinetti, Carrà and Russolo

24
Giacomo Balla
Rhythm of the Violinist 1912
Oil on canvas
52 × 75
(20½ × 29½)
Estorick Foundation, London

25
Anton Giulio Bragaglia
Balla in Front of 'Leash in Motion' 1912
Photograph
Antonella Vigliani Bragaglia Collection. Centro Studi Bragaglia, Rome

Balla, although a mentor to a number of the younger Futurists, was involved with the movement only at a distance during these early years. Based in Rome, he worked methodically during 1912 towards an art that sought to represent a scientific analysis of movement. During that year he accepted a commission to design furniture for, and to decorate the house of, Arthur and Grete Löwenstein in Düsseldorf. The unusual black and white v-shaped frame for his *Rhythm of the Violinist* 1912 (fig.24) suggests that the painting was part of this decorative scheme. Its effect on the composition is to emphasise the upward thrust of the violin, bow and musician's hands. The meticulously painted fine lines, extending, as it were, the dot of Divisionism to suggest movement, evoke a form of chronophotography. The inspiration for these works may well have been the photography of the theatre and film director Anton Giulio Bragaglia (1890–1960), who had photographed the artist the same year (fig.25), and his manifesto 'Futurist Photodynamism' (1911) as well as the famous pictures of the nineteenth-century photographers Eadweard Muybridge (fig.26) and Etienne-Jules Marey. Balla's analytical approach to the perception of external movement is not complicated by the memory traces, emotional forces and multiple viewpoints used by Boccioni and Carrà. It is, however, a complex organisation of brushstrokes that evidently suggests a musical analogy appropriate to the subject matter and gives a hint of Balla's interest in Symbolist and Theosophical ideas. In the same year Balla was also experimenting with a series

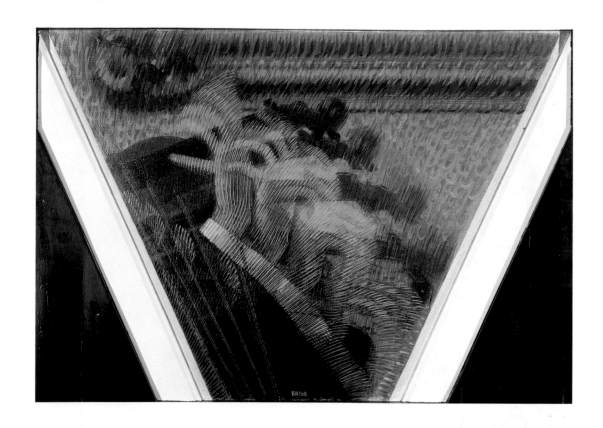

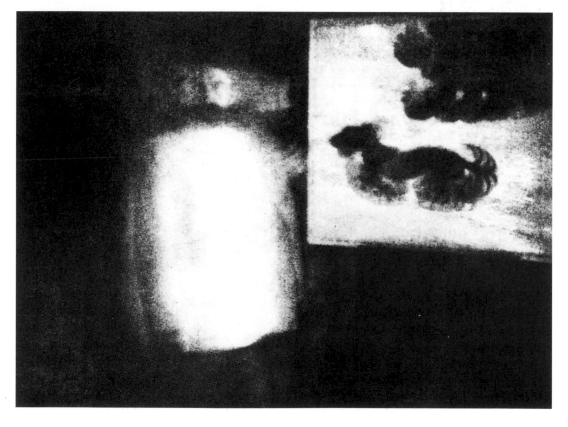

of abstract colour studies on paper and canvas, which were called *Iridescent Interpenetrations* (fig.27) and were closely related to this kind of painting and to his aesthetic theory. In these works coloured lozenges and other shapes are organised in geometrical patterns, similar to those found in the textbooks used by nineteenth-century artists such as Georges Seurat and the Italian Divisionists. Balla's intention, though, seems to have been to incite quasi-spiritual sensations in the viewer where the spectrum symbolises and effects a conjunction of complementaries, perhaps embodying Balla's response to the Futurists' demand for an 'innate complementariness' in the painter's vision. It is possible that Balla was also interested at this time in the works of the French painter Robert Delaunay whose *Windows* series (fig.28) similarly brought together scientific and mystical concerns with the power of colour.

In his sequence of paintings on the theme of abstract speed Balla became a fully fledged Futurist in his subject matter, observing, in his usual painstaking fashion, the movement of speeding cars and producing from a multitude of drawings a series of canvases in 1913 that were clearly intended to go beyond the more mechanically analytical works of the previous year. In *Abstract Speed: The*

Interpen26
Eadweard Muybridge

'Athletes Wrestling', reproduced in *Animal Locomotion* 1887

Victoria and Albert Museum

27
Giacomo Balla

Study for *Iridescent Interpenetration no.2* 1912

Watercolour on paper
22 × 18 (8¾ × 7)
Galleria Civica d'Arte Moderna, Turin

28
Robert Delaunay

Windows Open Simultaneously (First Part, Third Motif) 1912

Oil on canvas
45.7 × 37.5
(18 × 14¾)
Tate Gallery

29
Giacomo Balla

Abstract Speed: The Car Has Passed 1913

Oil on canvas
50.2 × 65.4
(19¾ × 25¾)
Tate Gallery

Car Has Passed (fig.29), part of a triptych, a simplified landscape provides a backdrop to a series of force lines tinged with the pink of exhaust traces that suggest the atmospheric disturbance caused by the now absent car of the central panel.

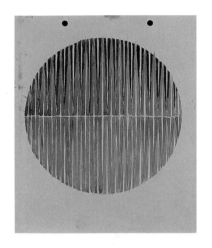

4

30
Giacomo Balla
Page from the 'Futurist
Manifesto of Men's
Clothing', 1913

THE FUTURIST RECONSTRUCTION OF THE UNIVERSE

Balla's overtly Futurist works coincided with an expansion of his interests in
1913 to include writing manifestos, experiments with language, theatre and
fashion design and sculpture (fig.30). As with Boccioni, his art was the focus for
an ambitious all-encompassing philosophy of Futurist life and his mission was
to redesign the world in Futurist mode:

> The consequent merry dazzle produced by our clothes in the noisy streets, which
> we shall have transformed with our Futurist architecture, will mean that
> everything will begin to sparkle like the glorious prison of a jeweller's gigantic
> glass-front, and all around us we shall find aerobatic blocks of colours set out like
> the following word-shapes:
>   Coffeeornhov Rosegreebastocap transpomotocar legcutshop
> blueblackwhitehouses aerocigarend skyroofliftyellight anomoviesphot
> barbebbenpurp.

Balla's vision here (from 'Futurist Manifesto of Men's Clothing') is that of an
avant-garde consumerism. His wordplay was part of a politically motivated
Futurist programme to disorientate and reorganise firstly Italian, and then all
human, experience through a radical disruption of ordinary language. Drawing
on late nineteenth-century French writers such as Stéphane Mallarmé and Jules
Laforgue and on contemporaries such as Apollinaire and Cendrars, Marinetti,
whose background was pre-eminently a literary one, had moved in his poetry,
prose, drama and polemical writing towards the concept of 'Words-in-
Freedom'. Turning his back on what he saw – for all their technical innovation –

as the flawed romantic sentimentality of his Symbolist forebears, Marinetti declared: 'To tears of beauty brooding tenderly over tombs, we oppose the keen, cutting profile of the pilot, the chauffeur, the aviator . . . We co-operate with Mechanics in destroying the old poetry of distance and wild solitudes, the exquisite nostalgia of parting, for which we substitute the tragic lyricism of ubiquity and omnipotent speed.'

Marinetti's 'Technical Manifesto of Futurist Literature' of 11 May 1912 set out a programme of syntactical revolution dictated, so he claimed, by the whirring propeller of his aeroplane as he flew over the rooftops and chimneys of Milan:

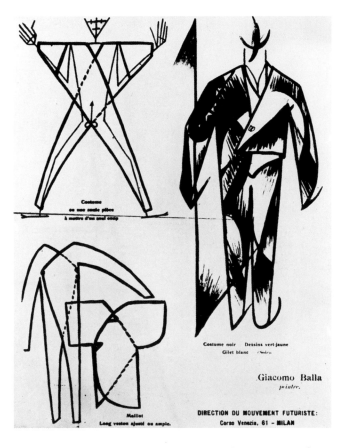

Costume
en une seule pièce
à mettre d'un seul coup

Costume noir   Dessins vert-jaune
Gilet blanc   (Noir).

Giacomo Balla
peintre.

Maillot
Long veston ajusté ou ample.

DIRECTION DU MOUVEMENT FUTURISTE:
Corso Venezia, 61 – MILAN

1. One must destroy syntax and scatter one's nouns at random, just as they are born.
2. One should use infinitives, because they adapt themselves elastically to nouns and don't subordinate them to the writer's 'I' that observed or imagined . . .
3. One must abolish the adjective, to allow the naked noun to preserve its essential colour . . .
4. One must abolish the adverb, old belt-buckle . . .
5. Every noun should have its double; that is, the noun should be followed, with no conjunction, by the noun to which it is related by analogy. Example: man-torpedo-boat, woman-gulf, crowd-surf, piazza-funnel . . .

He goes on to propose, among other iconoclastic gestures, the abolition of punctuation and its replacement with mathematics and musical symbols. One of his most important ideas was the extension and deepening of analogies, thus anticipating a Surrealist concept of writing: 'Analogy is nothing more than the deep love that assembles distant, seemingly diverse and hostile things . . . When, in my *Battle of Tripoli*, I compared a trench bristling with bayonets to an orchestra, a machine gun to a fatal woman, I intuitively introduced a large part of the universe into a short episode of African battle.' Underpinning these technical and imaginative transformations was a new, perhaps megalomaniac concept of subjectivity. Drawing on Bergson's ideas of intuition and matter, Marinetti proposes the destruction of the 'I', 'that is, all psychology . . . To capture the breath, the sensibility, and the instincts of free objects and whimsical motors'. At the heart of these ideas is a drive through 'divine intuition, the characteristic gift of the Latin races' to 'conquer the seemingly unconquerable hostility that separates out human flesh from the metal of motors'.

These literary and language-based concepts are fundamental to an understanding of Futurist ideology. In his manifesto 'Destruction of Syntax – Imagination with Strings – Words in Freedom' of 1913, Marinetti asserts that 'Futurism is grounded in the complete renewal of human sensibility brought about by the great discoveries of science'. He expands the earlier range of Futurist devices to include the 'semaphoric adjective', 'onomatopoeia', 'typographical revolution', 'multilinear lyricism' and 'free expressive orthography'. The effect of all these newly coined terms was to open up not just the purely semantic possibilities of language but also its profoundly visual dimension. The typographical experimentation of Marinetti's celebrated book *Zang Tumb Tumb* of 1914 (fig.31) was perhaps the most successful exercise in breaking down the barriers between words and images and thus in exploding the intricate edifice of conceptual distinctions upon which, Marinetti believed, the decadent effects of tradition and convention were based. Typically, it is inspired by war, notoriously described by Marinetti as 'the sole hygiene of the world', with a cover based on the forms of the shockwaves of high explosives and an aeroplane in flight. Marinetti had acted as a war reporter during the 1912 Balkan Wars and witnessed the Bulgarian siege of Adrianopolis in October of that year. By no means a simple glorification of war, *Zang Tumb Tumb* includes a sub-atomic account of the shocks he suffered under bombardment: 'I counted the 6 milliard shocks my molecule sisters gave me I obeyed them 6 milliard times taking 6 milliard different directions.' Futurist 'simultaneous' awareness is thus not only focused on the outside world's confusion of events and on the realm of personal memory but also on the invisible world of bodily experience. Not always successful, and certainly not entirely original, Marinetti's literary experiments were nevertheless a major development in the modernist project to reconfigure creativity, consciousness and aesthetic form in the light of the profound changes in technology and science that he had identified as the driving force in twentieth-century experience.

The Futurist visual artists, whose ideas had in fact fed into Marinetti's thinking, responded almost extravagantly in their art and writing to the challenge of the high stakes raised by this literary revolution. Carlo Carrà's manifesto 'The Painting of Sounds, Noises and Smells', published in the Florentine avant-garde magazine *Lacerba* in 1913, and perhaps indebted to

31
F.T. Marinetti
Cover of *Zang Tumb Tumb*, 1914
Tate Gallery Library

32
Umberto Boccioni
Unique Forms of Continuity in Space 1913, cast 1972
Bronze
117.5 × 87.6 × 36.8 (46 ¼ × 34 ½ × 14 ½)
Tate Gallery

Bragaglia's photographic theories, proposed that 'sounds, noises and smells are incorporated in the expression of lines, volumes and colours ... In railway stations and garages, and throughout the mechanical or sporting world, sound, noises and smells are predominantly red; in restaurants and cafés they are silver, yellow and blue, those of a woman are green, blue and violet.' Although it is a matter of faith as to whether these highly ambitious aims were achieved in any of Carrà's paintings or in those of his colleagues, the important point here is the concept of the expansion of the visual arts into areas of experience previously denied to them.

Boccioni's sculptures of 1912 and 1913 were translations into three dimensions of his evolving painterly concerns and further evidence of the broadening of the artist's horizons at this time. His theoretical writings, and the works they sought to explain in a dense, almost poetic prose, were perhaps the most complex and sophisticated synthesis of the broad Futurist theory of art and life with the ideas of Bergson and the demands of the plastic arts. The core of his theories was the notion of 'dynamism', which he explained as 'the lyrical conception of forms, interpreted in the infinite manifestations of the relativity between absolute motion and relative motion, between the environment and the object which come together to form the appearance of a whole: environment + object'. By 'absolute motion' Boccioni meant the invisible internal forces of an object, which the artist reveals in relation to its relative motion – that which it undergoes in movement through space. His sculpture *Unique Forms of Continuity in Space* 1913 (fig.32) bravely attempts to realise what he insisted were not 'crazy abstractions'. New minds could mean new bodies.

A number of earlier sculptures by Boccioni had rather literally combined the fragmented forms of a moving human figure with 'environmental' features such as houses and window frames. In accordance with his theories, atmosphere and space, object and force lines are transmitted one to the other, and thus by implication break down the barriers between subject and object. He had described his confused state while making these pieces in a letter to Severini (November 1912), with whom he had visited the studios of Alexander Archipenko, Constantine Brancusi and other Parisian sculptors: 'And then I am struggling with sculpture: I work work work and don't know what I am producing. Is it interior? Exterior? Is it sensation? Is it delirium? Is it mere brain? Analysis? Synthesis? What the hell it is I simply do not know! Forms on forms ... confusion.' Here is the authentic voice of the heroic Futurist, nearly deranged in his commitment to invention and the destruction of old formulae. Even Medardo Rosso, the pioneering Impressionist sculptor so much admired by the Futurists for his wax images of moving figures, was rejected by Boccioni as *passé* and too concerned with the discrete figure observed from one angle (fig.33).

Unique Forms of Continuity in Space was initially modelled in plaster and a number of bronzes were cast from this original many years after the artist's death. It is an almost baroque image of the man of the future, not only shown as a muscular form moving with awesome power through space, but also as a new type of being actually evolving through time into something beyond the human. Here, surely, is a statue, drawing heavily on the Hellenistic winged *Victory of Samothrace* in the Louvre, dedicated to Nietzsche's concept of the 'superman', who seems to become a semi-mechanised, bionic creature. If he could speak it would no doubt be in 'Words-in-Freedom'.

Futurism as an all-embracing movement in art and life, intent on 'a reconstruction of the universe' went far beyond painting and literature. Following Francesco Balilla Pratella's 'Manifesto of the Futurist Musicians' (1910), which had attacked *bel canto* and Italian opera and proclaimed the advent of atonality and irregular rhythms, Russolo published 'The Art of Noises' in 1913. He was proud of the fact that he was not a trained musician, claiming this

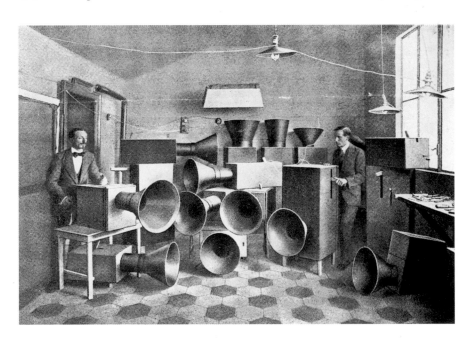

33
Medardo Rosso

Laughing Woman (Large Version)
*c.*1891, cast 1950s

Wax over plaster
54.5 × 51 × 19.2
(21½ × 20 × 7½)
Tate Gallery

34

Luigi Russolo and his assistant Ugo Piatti with Noise Intoners

would allow him to achieve a 'great renewal' of music through a response to the noises of the modern world:

> Let us cross a great modern capital with our ears more alert than our eyes, and we will get enjoyment from distinguishing the eddying of water, air and gas in metal pipes, the grumbling of noises that breathe and pulse with indisputable animality, the palpitation of valves, the coming and going of pistons, the howl of mechanical saws, the jolting of a tram on its rails, the cracking of whips, the flapping of curtains and flags.

While a number of late nineteenth- and early twentieth-century musicians had experimented with the relationship between colour and music – A.W. Rimington's 'Colour Music', Arnold Schoenberg's dialogue with the Expressionist painter Wassily Kandinsky, and the composer Alexander Scriabin's 'Colour Organ' being typical examples – Russolo's innovation was to go beyond conventional sources and techniques and, so to speak, 'tune-in' to the aural landscape of the modern world. To achieve his 'art of noise' Russolo devised a new form of notation and invented a range of machines that would reproduce the six varieties of noises he had defined in his manifesto. These *Intonarumori* (Noise Intoners) (fig.34) included 'Exploders', 'Cracklers', 'Gurglers', 'Buzzers' and 'Scrapers'. Russolo and his assistant Ugo Piatti toured Italy and other European countries and gave performances of works such as *The Awakening of a City* and *Meeting of Automobiles and Aeroplanes* to enraged, bemused and enthralled audiences. Russolo's extraordinary new music, which he continued to perform in the 1920s, had a dramatic effect on other composers

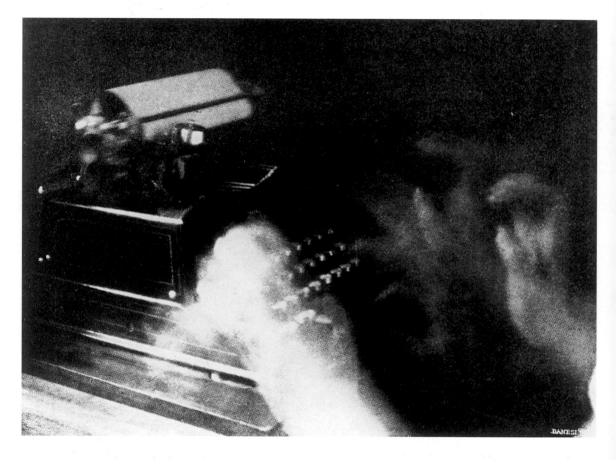

such as Igor Stravinsky, George Antheil, Arthur Honegger and Edgar Varèse. Sadly, none of his *Intonarumori* have survived.

We have seen the extent to which Balla responded to photography as a source for new approaches to painting. The fact is, however, that Boccioni, Carrà and other painters had shown little obvious interest in the camera and indeed were often actively hostile to it. Bragaglia's 'photodynamism', theoretically indebted to Bergsonian ideas of flux and synthesis, had been a bold attempt to use long exposures and other techniques to capture what he called the 'algebra of movement' and to convey an occult sense of the spiritual traces left by bodies in motion (fig.35). Bragaglia also referred to the possibility of evoking smells through photography, which he left mysteriously unexplained, but which nevertheless reminds us of the interest in the possibilities of synaesthesia among artists of this period. As with the painters and musicians, Bragaglia's version of Futurism was a movement that embraced modern technology, spiritual and paranormal phenomena and the concept of art integrated into life. Where Russolo sought to orchestrate industrial production, and Boccioni attempted urban symphonies of colour and movement, Bragaglia moved inevitably towards the most powerful art form of the twentieth century — cinema.

In 1916 Bragaglia, whose father had been an early pioneer of Italian cinema, set up his own film company and made four films. Only one of these has survived. With starkly geometrical backgrounds designed by Enrico Prampolini, *Thais* (1916) is a melodrama of tragic love and suicide in which dissolve effects, fragmentary captions of lines by Baudelaire and blue and

35
Anton Giulio Bragaglia

Typist 1911

Photograph
Antonella Vigliani
Bragaglia Collection.
Centro Studi Bragaglia,
Rome

36
Amaldo Ginna

Still from *Vita Futurista*
1916

orange colour toning evoke a claustrophobic atmosphere of emotional obsession.

In 1910 Arnaldo Ginna and his brother Bruno Corra painted colour on to four rolls of celluloid film untreated with silver nitrate. Inspired, in turn, by a painting of Giovanni Segantini, a song composed by Felix Mendelssohn, a poem by Mallarmé and the complementary colours red and green and blue and yellow, the two brothers were among a number of others, including Léopold Survage in Paris, who were finding remarkable possibilities in the new medium. In 1916, at the invitation of Marinetti and with the help of, among others, Balla and Emilio Settimelli, Ginna made the film *Vita Futurista*; although it is now lost, the surviving descriptions and stills (fig.36) suggest that it continued the attempt to use the movie camera in a way analogous to other forms of Futurist experimentation. Following the compressed acts and abrupt changes of Marinetti's Futurist Variety Theatre, the film is divided into episodes with titles such as 'How a Futurist Sleeps', 'Morning Gymnastics' and 'Futurist work'. Scenes within these episodes such as 'Balla falls in love with a chair and a footstool is born' and 'invasion of a passéist tea-party – conquest of women' indicate the slapstick and surreal character of the film, which Ginna claims was a nightmare to produce on account of the absurd and irresponsible behaviour of the Futurist actors. In spite of this, the evidence is that *Vita Futurista* constituted a remarkable moment in the early history of cinema. Using devices such as split screens, mirrors, bizarre combinations of objects and colour toning to evoke 'states of mind', Ginna and his anarchic colleagues sensed in the new technology of film an opportunity to realise the full ambition of Futurist ideas. Strangely, the promise of a Futurist cinematic *gesamtkunstwerk* was never realised. Other than fragmentary documentation, only the inspired and boastful manifestos and a legacy of avant-garde cinema by later film-makers bears witness to that promise: 'Thus we can break up and recompose the universe according to our marvellous whims, multiplying the force of the Italian creative genius and its absolute pre-eminence in the world.'

ARCHITECTURE

Futurist art, where it was concerned with the built environment, drew upon the urban realities of the great Italian cities such as Milan and Turin, which had grown rapidly during the late nineteenth century. This was a world of brick and stone embodied in traditional and classical forms. For Marinetti, however, it was not appropriate that the violent excitement of modern life should be projected onto such an anachronistic setting. The setting needed to be recreated. Firstly, inevitably, there had to be a total destruction of the old cityscape. As early as April 1910 Marinetti and his accomplices had thrown, it was claimed, nearly a million leaflets, 'Against Passéist Venice', from the top of St Mark's campanile and on to a passing crowd below:

> Let us burn the gondolas, rocking chairs for Cretins and raise to the heavens the imposing geometry of metal bridges and howitzers plumed with smoke, to abolish the falling curves of the old architecture.
> Let the reign of holy Electric Light finally come, to liberate Venice from its venal moonshine of furnished rooms.

Marinetti bellowed an improvised speech at the crowd, denouncing the decline of Venice, while his supporters, including Boccioni, Russolo and Carrà, applauded him and involved themselves in skirmishes with angry opponents, excited and angered by the Futurists' provocations.

The next, more difficult stage would be the creation of Futurist cities. While Carrà and Boccioni had hinted in their manifestos at the need for a new kind of architecture, their ideas, inevitably, were founded in their practices as painters and lacked the focus necessary for a radical departure in building and urban planning. It was a young Milanese architect, Antonio Sant'Elia (1888–1916), an ex-employee of the Technical Office of Milan's City Council, who provided the vision. Influenced initially by Viennese modernists such as Otto Wagner and

37
Antonio Sant'Elia
Electric Power Plant
1914

Pencil and inks on paper
31 × 20.5
(12¼ × 8)
Private Collection

Adolf Loos, Sant'Elia had formed a group of architects, 'Nuove Tendenza' (New Tendency), whose first major exhibition was held at the Famiglia Artistica in May 1914. The drawings by Sant'Elia (fig.37) and his friends, such as the Swiss architect Mario Chiattone, marked a dramatic change in their aesthetic from an elaborately decorative Art Nouveau style to a streamlined modernity where the vertical straight line defined the energy and severity of the 'New City', soon to become the 'Futurist City'. Impossibly utopian as they were, the drawings powerfully expressed a new aesthetic and contained the seeds of a social and political vision in tune with Marinetti's polemics.

Sant'Elia's skyscrapers, railway stations, power stations and airfields (envisaged in steel, reinforced concrete, plate glass, cardboard and other new materials) were part of an integrated plan for the corporate rationalisation of modern Italy. All forms of energy, natural and human, would be harnessed into an ever-changing power-house of a multi-level city which, in its dynamic structure, would deny the past's stranglehold over change. Sant'Elia aimed at an impermanent, renewable architecture, fully in accord with Bergsonian concepts of creative evolution and Marinetti's demand for perpetual revolutionary transformation.

Sant'Elia's 'Manifesto of Futurist Architecture', published in *Lacerba* in August 1914, and almost certainly edited by Marinetti, begins by conducting the usual assault on the past and on current practice, and by asserting the need to confront the urgent realities of the present. Above all, these realities were new materials and new patterns of life: 'We must invent and rebuild the Futurist city like an immense and tumultuous shipyard, agile, mobile and dynamic in every detail; and the Futurist house must be like a gigantic machine.' Anticipating Le Corbusier's concept of the house as a 'machine for living in', Sant'Elia describes, in effect, a fantastic redevelopment of an American city such as New York, where decoration is abolished, skyscrapers dominate and life is recognised as a dizzying synthesis of vertical and horizontal forces: 'the street will no longer lie like a doormat at ground level, but will plunge many storeys down into the earth, embracing the metropolitan traffic, and will be linked up for necessary interconnections by metal gangways and swift-moving pavements.' It was part of the Futurist faith that Italy should look towards America for inspiration rather than to Europe. At an ideological level, however, the Futurist city, dubbed 'Milano 2,000' by Sant'Elia, was at odds with American individualism, for it sought to control and to harmonise human life in a quasi-totalitarian structure. Whatever Sant'Elia's rhetoric about new freedoms and the expression of the spirit, his vision anticipates the authoritarian fantasies of Mussolini's Fascist mass society. Sant'Elia's drawings, perhaps ominously, rarely include human figures

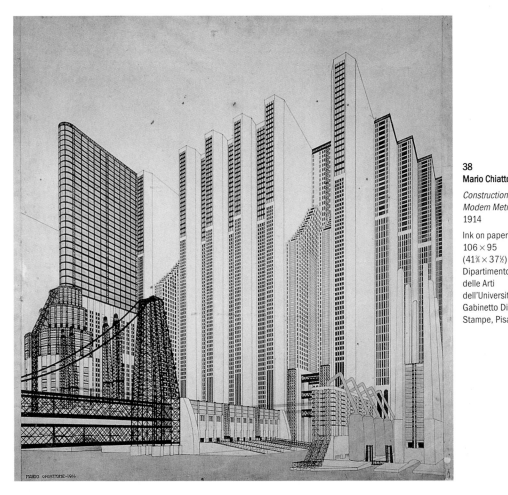

38
Mario Chiattone

Construction for a Modern Metropolis
1914

Ink on paper
106 × 95
(41¾ × 37½)
Dipartimento di Storia delle Arti dell'Università, Gabinetto Disegni e Stampe, Pisa

and show a mechanised world disconnected from nature. Transport systems, living quarters and industrial areas are brought together in a complex series of relations in which people are effectively productive and communicative units in a monumental circulation of forces. In a sense, the human being has been fully absorbed into the dynamic field of Futurist painting. This sci-fi unreality is accentuated in Chiattone's drawings of the 'modern metropolis' (fig.38) where the quality of artificially lit stage scenery anticipates the spectacular scenography of Fascist ceremonial architecture.

FUTURISM ON THE ROAD

Marinetti, who called himself 'the caffeine of Europe', spread the word about Futurism across the continent through exhibitions, performances, events, pamphlets, publicity stunts and a shrewd manipulation of the press. By the outbreak of the First World War, Futurism was a household name throughout Europe and had even gained a foothold in the United States and in Brazil and Mexico. Synonymous with outrage, violence, novelty and excitement, it was by far the most visible face of an international avant-garde that was otherwise largely unknown to, and certainly little understood by, the great mass of people. It is not possible in a study of this length to examine the extraordinary extent of the international impact of Futurism; rather we will look briefly and highly selectively at that impact in two contrasting contexts – Britain and Russia.

'THE GREAT VORTEX': FUTURISM AND VORTICISM IN LONDON

The response to Futurism among young artists in London eventually led to the formation of the Vorticist movement which, while heavily indebted to many aspects of the Italian group's ideas and practices, was also fiercely and critically independent. English audiences had been introduced to post-Impressionist painting through two exhibitions organised in 1910 and 1912 in London by the critic and painter Roger Fry. By Futurist or Cubist standards, Fry's exhibitions were tame and uncontroversial but had nevertheless fascinated and alarmed many through their display of works by Paul Cézanne, Paul Gauguin, Henri

Matisse and others. When the same British audience was confronted in 1912 by the first Futurist Exhibition at the Sackville Gallery in the West End, it was still more astonished, even horrified, by what it saw as the excesses of the new tendencies in European art. With the various turbulent Futurist events organised to publicise the Italians' presence in London, and the political issues of Ulster, the suffragettes and syndicalist-inspired strikes in the major industries, a fairly conservative public may well have felt that they had good reason to be concerned about the provocatively novel and seemingly deliberately ugly and discordant art of the Futurists. Many would have been unimpressed by Marinetti's preparatory speech delivered at the Lyceum Club in 1910 in which he chided them for 'the dismal, ridiculous condemnation of Oscar Wilde. Intellectual Europe will never forgive you for it.'

Marinetti made strenuous efforts to recruit support among the avant-garde in London but had only very limited success. He was certainly an important catalyst in 1912 and 1913 in generating debate and experiment among artists and writers but his sole committed supporter in London, the painter Christopher Nevinson, who had studied at the Slade School of Art and in Paris, was ostracised by his peers when he signed the 'Vital English Art: Futurist Manifesto' in 1914 at Marinetti's instigation. Nevinson had met Severini at the Sackville exhibition and had travelled with him to Paris where he was introduced to Boccioni, Apollinaire and others. The impact of his introduction to Futurism and the scene in Paris was immediate and dramatic. His work, already often concerned with contemporary urban scenes and modern life in general, focused in paintings such as *The Arrival* (fig.39) on movement, fragmented form and the romance of travel.

39
Christopher Richard Wynne Nevinson
*The Arrival c.*1913
Oil on canvas
76.2 × 63.5 (30 × 25)
Tate Gallery

40
Wyndham Lewis
Print from portfolio
Timon of Athens 1912
Tate Gallery Library

In Wyndham Lewis (1882–1957), painter, writer and the leading figure of the Vorticist movement, Marinetti came up against a rival of remarkable talent and intellect. Lewis had trained at the Slade School of Art at the turn of the century and travelled extensively in Europe from Brittany to Munich, Paris to Madrid. By the time he resettled in London in 1909 he had acquainted himself with the main intellectual and artistic currents in France and Germany and had developed his own aesthetic philosophy. Influenced by writers such as the anarchist Max Stirner and by Nietzsche, he was also familiar with Cubist and Expressionist art.

There is little doubt that Lewis was highly receptive to Futurist ideas and art, and works such as his illustrations of 1912 to Shakespeare's *Timon of Athens*

(fig.40) show a marked affinity with Boccioni's output during this period. However, Lewis's art is more severely geometrical and lacks the loosely turbulent psychological atmosphere evoked by Boccioni, whose aim was to convey a sense of real movement. Lewis rejected the Futurist obsession with what he saw as the trappings of modernity and the romance of speed, and in his work placed the emphasis instead on surface and form.

By 1914 Lewis had gathered around himself a loosely allied group of like-minded artists and, along with the American poet Ezra Pound (1885–1972) and a wealthy supporter Kate Lechmere, founded the Rebel Art Centre, a group defined partly by rivalry with the Bloomsbury artists of the Omega Workshops such as Vanessa Bell, Duncan Grant and Roger Fry. The Rebel Art Centre did not survive long but was the crucible in which Vorticism was created. The image of the vortex was intended to convey a sense of dynamism but one at odds with what the English artists saw as, in Pound's phrase, the 'accelerated impressionism' of Futurism. The vortex has a still centre around which form is organised, and by this Lewis and his associates meant partly to suggest that Futurism was undisciplined and superficial. Lewis and Pound, in particular, were keen students of Chinese and Japanese art and saw analogies between their work and oriental painting and aesthetic theory. Deeply committed to an engagement with the spirit of contemporary life, they nevertheless stressed the need for detachment and were unimpressed with the heroic immersion in matter and movement that was so central to Futurist thinking. Although both men were also interested in the anarchist and radical politics espoused by the Italians, they made it a requirement that the artist remain aloof from the sphere of action and insisted on the autonomy of art.

The journal *Blast*, which first appeared in July 1914 was the Vorticists' attempt to take on the tactics of the classic Futurist manifesto and to develop Marinetti's typographical experiments (fig.42). Where the Futurists used their varied typefaces in a spirit of wayward polemic, often effacing the difference between text and image, the *Blast* manifestos are almost architectural in their organisation and perhaps emulate the style of the popular newspaper or billboard. While there is a strong nationalistic tone at work in *Blast*, particularly through contrasts with French and Italian culture, there is, equally, a satirical attack on British assumptions, snobbery and complacency. In the same spirit that Marinetti had attacked Italian 'passéism', so the pages of *Blast* contain a series of attacks on the English climate, aestheticism, humour, sport, and Victorian middle-class values. On the other hand, England is 'blessed' for its maritime and industrial power and for its tradition of satire. This dialectical approach knowingly creates a gap in which the Vorticist vision is intended to emerge: 'We start from opposite statements of a chosen world. Set up violent structure of adolescent clearness between two extremes.'

41
Wyndham Lewis

Vortex symbol, reproduced in *Blast: Review of the Great English Vortex*, no.1, 1914, edited by Wyndham Lewis

42
Page from *Blast: Review of the Great English Vortex*, no.1, 1914

The polemical attacks by the Vorticists on Futurism (or as they dubbed it, 'automobilism') drew on their belief that the Bergsonian emphasis on life and the flux of time was at odds with art's focused presence. Pound wrote: 'Futurism is the disgorging spray of a vortex with no drive behind it, DISPERSAL.'

The vortex symbol that appears in *Blast* (fig.41) suggests an elaborate reference to the ideological position of the English artists and carries strong nationalist and racial overtones. It has been persuasively argued that the curious inverted lampshade-like form is based on a nautical storm-cone. These canvas objects were used on ships to indicate the direction of storms, controlled by a rope that made them point either up or down. A storm-cone pointing up warned of a storm coming from the north. Thus the suggestion of this secret emblem is that Vorticism is a northern European cultural storm directed against the Mediterranean gales of Futurism. 'Let us once more wear the ermine of the north', exclaims the opening manifesto. Lewis frequently pointed out that England was the home of the industrial revolution and that she had no need of the sentimental 'hysterics' of excitable 'Latin-types' for whom economic upheaval was a far more recent experience. England, 'Industrial island machine', proud of its seafarers and ports with 'heavy insect dredgers', was the home of Jonathan Swift with his 'solemn bleak wisdom of laughter' and of 'the British Grin'.

Lewis's particular notion of human life was based on the idea of dualism, or the radical divorce of mind and body. For him the mind, no matter what science might say and the Futurists urge, was at war with the body. This belief meant that he held to an utterly sceptical view of the political action that provided the main impulse for Futurism. Where Marinetti, Boccioni and their colleagues enthused about the loss of self in the crowd and the identification with matter in a sort of ecstasy of communication with the life-force, Lewis cautioned in favour of individual, indeed deliberately ego-centred, self-reliance, eyes fixed on the present rather than the future.

While few of Lewis's major Vorticist canvases survive, many works on paper still exist. These show that by 1914 he, like his fellow Vorticists, was engaged with abstraction. There are, however, few entirely non-representational works. His monumental canvas *The Crowd* of 1914–15 (fig.44) shows how he worked

1

BLAST First (from politeness) **ENGLAND**

CURSE ITS CLIMATE FOR ITS SINS AND INFECTIONS

DISMAL SYMBOL, SET round our bodies, of effeminate lout within.

VICTORIAN VAMPIRE, the **LONDON** cloud sucks the TOWN'S heart.

A 1000 MILE LONG, 2 KILOMETER Deep

BODY OF WATER even, is pushed against us from the Floridas, **TO MAKE US MILD.**

OFFICIOUS MOUNTAINS keep back **DRASTIC WINDS**

SO MUCH VAST MACHINERY TO PRODUCE

THE CURATE of "Eltham"
BRITANNIC ÆSTHETE
WILD NATURE CRANK
DOMESTICATED
        POLICEMAN
LONDON COLISEUM
  SOCIALIST-PLAYWRIGHT
DALY'S MUSICAL COMEDY
GAIETY CHORUS GIRL
TONKS

between a highly formalised approach and the demands of representation without which, he believed, art could have no powerful significance. The painting is also a critique of Futurist art and political ideology. In the bottom left-hand corner a number of large robotic figures, gathered near a French national flag, appear to be opening or closing a door separating them from a cityscape, which dominates the picture. Between the interstices of this schematic representation of city buildings, and across wide open spaces, move beehive-like configurations of figures, suggestive of mobile political groups – one of the protagonists holds a prominent red flag. The regimented phalanxes appear to be moving towards the top right hand corner of the painting where more compact groups of figures are perhaps at work in a factory, suggested by curved shapes.

Whether or not *The Crowd* refers to an actual event in French political history, recent or otherwise, has not been established. It is likely that it was painted after the outbreak of the First World War in August 1914: 'The Crowd Master', a story by Lewis in the second issue of *Blast*, which appeared in June 1915, gives an account of the masses in London gathering in the immediate lead-up to the declaration of war. Lewis equates the crowd with war and death and the individual with peace: 'The Crowd is an immense anaesthetic towards death.' Such sentiments, as we shall see, could hardly be further from the attitude of the Futurists who violently encouraged Italy's entry into the war on the allied side in 1915. It is extremely likely that Lewis, who was moving towards a rather maverick conservatism during this period, was also influenced in his choice of subject matter by the writing of the right-wing French sociologist Gustave Le Bon. Le Bon's book *The Psychology of Crowds*, published in 1895 and translated into English the following year (though Lewis read French fluently), analysed the psychology of crowd behaviour and was highly influential on thinkers from Freud to Hitler at the beginning of the century. Le Bon, an anti-democrat, saw humans as psychologically weak and easily manipulated through education, political propaganda and other means. Most individuals, claimed Le Bon, easily surrendered their independence to the will of organised elites and happily merged their interests with those of the multitude. With this merging of the self, obviously, came loss of responsibility. Le Bon's argument is a complex one but clearly made many telling points about human psychology and modern mass societies. *The Crowd* similarly presents social and political life as an ominous and alien sphere from which the artist, at least, needed to remain detached. It represents, so to speak, the politics of

43
Edward Wadsworth

*The Port c.*1915

Woodcut on paper
18.7 × 12.7
(7¼ × 5)
Tate Gallery

44
Wyndham Lewis

The Crowd 1914–15

Oil on canvas
200.7 × 153.7
(79 × 60½)
Tate Gallery

disengagement, where Russolo's *Revolt*, for example, had urged engagement.

Although the Vorticists were a less unified group and were certainly less politically grounded than the Futurists, there was among their varied work a broadly shared aesthetic. Edward Wadsworth, who came from a wealthy, northern, industrial family and who had trained first as an engineer and then, in Munich and London as a painter, was close to Lewis (the two, for instance, went on walking holidays in Yorkshire). His series of woodcuts of industrial

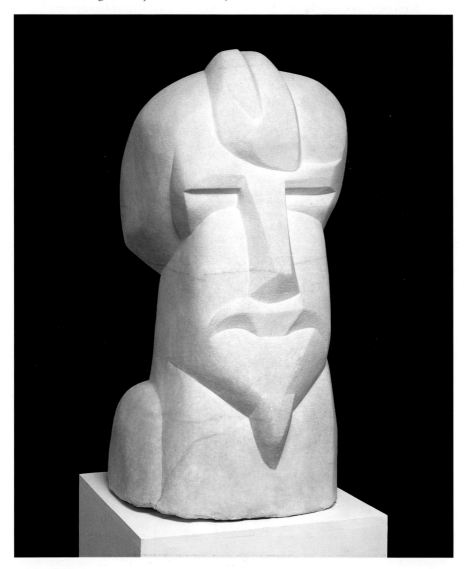

England displayed extraordinary delicacy and compactness of form. Vorticism demanded a geometrical and condensed translation of the perceived world and Wadsworth's work of this period was among the most original and successful. Lewis noted this quality in one of Wadsworth's port scenes, praising 'its white excitement, and compression of clean metallic shapes in the well of the harbour, as though in a broken cannon-mouth' (fig.43).

Vorticism had grown partly from its literary counterpart, Imagism. Two leading figures of Imagism, Ezra Pound and the philosopher, critic and poet T.E. Hulme, were closely involved in the contemporary debates in London about art and poetry, and were instrumental in the formation of the new aesthetic.

Pound, as has been mentioned, was deeply influenced by oriental poetry and had made a particular study of the Chinese ideogram. He formed a close relationship with the young French sculptor Henri Gaudier-Brzeska who had moved to London in 1908 and whose ink drawings show the influence of oriental calligraphy, no doubt reflecting the interests of his American friend. Gaudier's marble *Hieratic Head of Ezra Pound* (fig.45), carved in his studio under a railway arch at Putney Bridge in 1914, indicates the mix of primitivism, shamanism and modernist geometry typical of his work at this time. In profile the sculpture is unmistakably a phallus, presenting Pound as a source of creative power and poets in general as 'antennae of the race', as the American believed. The sharp, geometrical planes and compacted forms of the sculpture share with Futurist art a certain modernity, which is then contradicted by strong archaic resonances.

45
Henri Gaudier-Brzeska
Hieratic Head of Ezra Pound 1914

Marble
91.4 × 48 × 42
(36 × 19 × 16½)
Courtesy Anthony
d'Offay Gallery, London

46
Jacob Epstein
Doves 1914–15

Greek marble
64.8 × 78.7 × 34.3
(25½ × 31 × 13½)
Tate Gallery

The same quality of streamlined primeval forces is evident in the sculpture of the American, Jacob Epstein, who had settled in London in 1905. His carving *Doves* (fig.46) compresses an act of copulation into a compact shape highly suggestive of some streamlined mechanical form – a strange variation on the theme of sex-machine! Epstein's work was particularly admired by T.E. Hulme, who had translated Bergson into English, as well as the writings of the French syndicalist Georges Sorel. In seeking to explain the importance of Epstein's sculpture Hulme drew on the writings of the German philosopher of art Wilhelm Worringer. Worringer argued that there were two kinds of art – the abstract and the naturalistic. While the latter, typified by Greek and Renaissance art, depended upon a humanist sensibility and empathy with the body, the abstract, as found in Egyptian and Oceanic art for instance, was rooted in a deep fear of nature. The flowing forms of naturalistic art were denied by the harsh geometry of abstract art as the latter sought to impose order on the arbitrary and temporal life of the natural world. Hulme, citing artists such as Epstein as evidence, proposed that European art was entering a new phase of abstraction and that a concomitant social order based on hierarchy and tradition was imminent. Thus, while the Italian Futurists saw in the machine age auguries of almost wild human emancipation through technology, Hulme, and a number of the Vorticists, saw machinery and the art of the engineer's drawing as the signs of an extraordinary authoritarian modernism emerging in the culture of their time.

BEYOND REASON: FUTURISM IN RUSSIA

We have seen that Futurism, a term that for many during the second decade of the century was virtually synonymous with 'avant-garde', and therefore often imprecisely used, was both an international and a nationalist phenomenon. It was international in the way that avant-garde culture inevitably was in this period on account of the promiscuous mobility of the ideas of its protagonists; it was nationalist, as is clear in the case of Italy's relationship with

Britain, and in the drive to find an 'authentic' culture of new or revived nationhood. The cultural geography of Futurism in the wider context of the avant-garde, then, is a highly significant factor in our understanding of its role in European history prior to the outbreak of the First World War.

In the case of Russian 'Futurism', a label that should be viewed with some caution, these questions of cultural interchange are especially important because they also involve a broader issue about 'east' and 'west', the 'oriental'

Cézanne and the Cubists to an aerial and, finally, a cosmic world freed from the gravity of Suprematism. Much influenced by the ideas of contemporary occult writers such as P.D. Ouspensky about the fourth dimension , Malevich, as it were, rewrote art history to put himself in the vanguard not just of a new art but of a new consciousness and, indeed, a new universe. Extreme as his claims may seem, his tactics were not unique!

In Britain and Russia, therefore, there were important and vigorous responses to Italian Futurism. The artists of these countries were not in thrall to Marinetti's group – although they often underplayed its significance and originality – but their responses to it revealed its fertile and suggestive

50
Kasimir Malevich

An Englishman in Moscow 1914

Oil on canvas 88 × 57
(34½ × 22½)
Stedelijk Museum,
Amsterdam

51
Kasimir Malevich

Dynamic Suprematism
1915 or 1916

Oil on canvas
80.3 × 80 (31½ × 31½)
Tate Gallery

expansiveness. The same can be said of artists in many other countries at this time including Germany, France, Poland, Hungary and the United States. Italian Futurism, for all its aesthetic and political flaws, its pretentious claims and glory-snatching, was a truly seminal force that crossed national and artistic boundaries with mischievous and arrogant ease.

6

52
Gino Severini

The Hospital Train
1915

Oil on canvas
117 × 90 (46 × 35½)
Stedelijk Museum,
Amsterdam

'WAR: SOLE HYGIENE OF THE WORLD'

Futurism celebrated war. When it finally came to Europe in August 1914 Marinetti and his followers, unsurprisingly, urged Italians to join the allied side against the Germans and Austro-Hungarians with whom Italy at the time had a triple alliance. Futurist manifestos and closely, if uneasily, aligned journals such as *Lacerba* described the choice facing the nation as a cultural one where Giolliti's neutrality was not an option and heroic sacrifice was a duty. War was seen as a final glorious synthesis of all the forces pushing Italy towards 'Panitalianism' and modernisation. Violent demonstrations were staged in various Italian cities, Balla designed 'anti-neutral' clothing, Austrian flags were burned, fights with pacifists led to riots and, for extremists such as Boccioni, nights were spent in jail. Leaflets were distributed, such as the 'Futurist Synthesis of War' of September 1914 with Carrà's conceptual diagram setting the forces of progress, including Italy, England and France, against the *passatismo* (past-mindedness) of the hated Austrians and Germans. At the heart of this Bergsonian battle between life and invention, on the one hand, and rigidity and analysis, on the other, was the power of *Futurismo*, the embodiment, simultaneously, of the will-to-power, anarchist internationalism and historical nationalism.

During this period the interventionist Futurist 'Political Action Theatre' was created. That it was a cause of only mild concern for the authorities, however, is shown by this extract from a document sent by the Prefect of Milan to the Public Security Office in Rome following an 'event' at the Teatro del Verme during the premiere of Puccini's opera *Fanciulla dello West* on 15 September 1914:

'After the first act of the opera, the well-known Marinetti unrolled from the upper circle an Italian flag and shouted "Long Live Italy and France". At the same time, from another gallery, the Futurist Carrà waved what looked not like a flag, but some formless cloth of tiny dimension, tinted in two colours, yellow and black, which he then tore into pieces. The large audience was busy applauding the artists and Maestro Puccini, who were just taking their curtain call, and were nearly oblivious to the action ... The whole thing was a totally isolated case and was carried out by individuals, who did not find the slightest following in the audience.' Marinetti seems to have had greater success inflaming the patriotic passions of young students by interrupting lectures at universities, and of the working classes when he demonstrated support for France alongside the socialist leader Benito Mussolini in 1915. Believing that he had persuaded the previously pacifist Mussolini to side with the 'interventionist' cause, he claimed him also as a convert to Futurism. Art, he convinced himself, had merged with political action.

Finally, Italy entered the war in May 1915 and many of the Futurists were quick to volunteer for active service. Marinetti, along with his Milanese supporters, Boccioni, Russolo, Sant'Elia, Ugo Piatti and Mario Sironi joined the short-lived Lombard volunteer Cyclist Battalion in July 1915 and saw action in the vicious fighting in the Trentino. In spite of the military commitments of the movement, Marinetti kept Futurism alive during the war through 'action theatre' supporting the war effort, and by encouraging his artists to respond to the 'splendour of the conflagration'. He had written to Severini in Paris in November 1914: 'Try to live the war pictorially, studying it in all its marvellous mechanical forms (military trains, fortifications, wounded men, ambulances, hospitals, parades, etc.).' Severini took Marinetti's advice and, although he was hardly a belligerent enthusiast for war, he produced a series of images of armoured and hospital trains (fig.52) moving through Paris, through which he aimed to create what he termed 'Symbols of War': 'A few objects, or a few forms that related to a certain reality, perceived in their "essential state" as "pure notion", provided me with a highly condensed and extremely modern idea-image of war.' These paintings were shown at an exhibition of Futurist war

53
Carlo Carrà

Interventionist Manifesto 1914

Collage on paste-board
38 × 30
(15 × 11¾)
Collection Mattioli,
Milan

54
Carlo Carrà

The Drunken Gentleman 1916

Oil on canvas
60 × 45
(23¾ × 17¾)
Private Collection

art in Paris in 1916 and the lecture that Severini gave during the display formed the basis of two articles in the *Mercure de France*. The significance of these articles is that they demonstrated a profound shift in Severini's aesthetic thinking, which matches similar fundamental changes of outlook in Boccioni and Carrà. In effect, Severini was moving towards a rationalist reworking of tradition and figuration and away from the disrupted and dynamic forms of Futurism in its heroic years. In this he can be seen as part of the 'return to order', which many European artists, as varied as Picasso, Wyndham Lewis and Carrà, were undergoing during and after the war.

Carrà had been moving away from 'Marinettism', as it was dubbed by

detractors, and had spent much time in Paris during 1914. His correspondence with Severini shows that both artists were contemptuous of what Carrà called 'the dung-heap of social humanitarian sentimentality'. The wonderful exuberance of Carrà's 'interventionist' work, made upon his return to Italy at the end of 1914, however, shows that temporarily he was caught up in the patriotic fervour of the time and was subject to the 'sentimentality' he professed to despise: 'For me love of the fatherland was a moral entity and could not be considered as an abstraction but as a spiritual force.' His *Interventionist Manifesto* (fig.53) is a frenetic collage that uses a spiral composition to draw the spectator into a maelstrom of words, letters, colours and fragmented form suggestive of a propeller shredding newspapers. Following his earlier idea of painting noises, Carrà's 'plastic abstraction of civil tumult',

as he describedthis piece, celebrates Italy, its aviators, the noises of war, Marinetti and other heroes of the modern movement. This kind of aestheticised propaganda was to have a deep influence on Dada artists such as Kurt Schwitters a few years later.

Such works, though, were a lively interruption to a general trend in Carrà's art satisfying what he called 'a need that had matured in me for something different and more measured ... a strong desire to identify my painting with history, and particularly with Italian art history'. Like Severini, he was drawn towards his own artistic heritage – Giotto, Uccello and other early Renaissance Italian artists, whose work he interpreted as a peculiarly Italian expression of a sense of gravity, solidarity and mystery. As with Futurism, Carrà's new art stemmed from a powerful sense of national identity, but it is as if having been part of a race towards modernisation he was now drawn to deeper aesthetic roots at odds with the excitability and fragmentation of Marinetti's vision. When he was called up to the infantry in 1917 Carrà was diagnosed mentally ill and eventually went to a military hospital in Ferrara where he met the Italian painter Giorgio de Chirico. De Chirico, who had no time for Futurism, had spent a number of years before the war in Paris where he had invented a way of painting that had anticipated Carrà's own interests and was to have a major impact on the development of Surrealism after the war. The two men coined the term 'Metaphysical Painting' to describe the work they produced during

their brief partnership (fig.54). By 'metaphysical' they meant to suggest almost the opposite of what Futurism stood for: instead of movement, stillness; instead of fragmentation, structure; instead of interaction, separation. Whereas Futurism had stressed an immersion of the self in the dynamic flow of life and pushed art to polemical extremes, Carrà and de Chirico sought detachment, mental poise and simplicity. In some ways the two movements were dialectical partners within the complex changes in Italian culture that we have been examining. The tension between dynamism and classical order was to be a key theme throughout the Fascist era in Italy.

Boccioni, perhaps Marinetti's most loyal supporter, was killed in August 1916 when he was thrown off a horse while training with an artillery regiment near Verona. His diary records his excitement and fear during combat, in prose worthy of Marinetti: 'Zuiii Zuiii Tan Tan. Bullets all around. Volunteers calm on the ground shoot Pan Pan. Crack shot Sergeant Massai on his feet shoots, first shrapnel explodes.' He also records his heroic attitude for posterity: 'Now the lieutenant comes and tells me to stay behind because my cough is dangerous for everybody at night in a surprise action . . . I protest with energy I would rather quit the corps than stay behind, "I'll cough with my head in a blanket but I want to be in the front line!"'

Curiously, little of his art is in tune with these experiences and the major war image of this period, *Lancer's Charge* (fig.55), was a collage made towards the end of 1914 before Italy entered the war. Over newspaper cuttings describing French advances against the Germans in Alsace, a row of mounted soldiers painted in

tempera attacks a group of German soldiers in a trench at the bottom left. The work is one of Boccioni's last clearly Futurist pieces and during 1915 and 1916 he began a reinterpretation of Cézanne which, although quite distinct from the direction taken by Severini or Carrà, showed a renewed concern with a more structured and sculptural approach. One of his last major paintings was a portrait of the Italian composer Ferruccio Busoni (fig.56) who had been one of the first buyers of his works. It was made in 1916 while the two men were staying at the villa of the marchese and marchesa in Pallanza in Lake Maggiore. A portrait commission may not give an accurate indication of Boccioni's true direction at this point but, along with other contemporary works, there is a marked concern with the legacy of Cézanne. Boccioni, however, did not aspire to an inert museum art and his late writings on art suggest a continuing commitment to chromatic luminosity and an underlying sense of dynamism within the material world.

7

DEDICATED FOLLOWERS OF FASCISM:
SECOND FUTURISM, *AEROPITTURA* AND MUSSOLINI

By the end of 1916, with the death and departure from the movement of many of its key figures, the first period of Futurism was at an end. Marinetti, however, kept the movement alive by organising Futurist 'Synthetic Theatre' events, commissioning the film *Vita Futurista*, giving lectures, publishing, and looking for new recruits to the cause. Throughout, he was single-minded in his commitment to the war, a sentiment not shared by the majority of his fellow countrymen. By 1917, and after the humiliating defeat at Caporetto, most Italians were sick of the conflict and looked for scapegoats among the politicians, industrial magnates and military leaders whom they blamed for their devastated condition.

Newly formed combatants' organisations became a fertile breeding ground for Fascism exploited by Mussolini following his expulsion from the Socialist Party. There was much talk of the 'avant-garde of those who return from the front', who would instinctively know how to rejuvenate Italy at a time of national crisis. The solidarity of the servicemen was described as a *fascio combatto* (compact bundle), an image that became more potent and threatening to the government as the country collapsed into political and economic disorder at the end of the war. Mussolini deliberately called his new movement, launched in March 1919, *Fasci di Combattimento* in order to appeal to the four million ex-servicemen he believed would form the solid core of his support. In fact this bid was initially unsuccessful and Mussolini's first followers were the middle-class officers and administrators who felt they had lost the most following demobilisation; the *Arditi* (Daring Ones), or elite stormtroopers of the army, who were attracted to violent political action; and the *Fasci Politici Futuristi*, who were, in effect, military followers of Marinetti and who formed the basis of the Futurist Political Party that had been launched in 1918. The latter's programme called for 'revolutionary nationalism', 'obligatory gymnastics, sport and military education in the open air', proportional representation, abolition of the monarchy, easy divorce, equal pay for women, 'socialisation of the land' and a host of other radical measures designed to sustain the Futurist pre-war vision in a time of dramatic upheaval and political opportunity. Marinetti was particularly keen to forge an alliance with the *Arditi*, whom he saw as the 'Men of the Future', as one leaflet put it: 'the Futurist at war, the bohemian avant-garde ready for everything, light-hearted, agile, unbridled; the gay power of a twenty-year old youth who throws a bomb while whistling a song from a variety show.'

For the next few years Marinetti pursued an idiosyncratic path through the complex web of Italian politics that formed the prelude to Mussolini's 'March on Rome' in 1922. While sympathetic to many aspects of extreme left-wing thought, he was ideologically opposed to the Marxist dogma of class struggle. It was Mussolini and Fascism, however, that Marinetti tracked most closely, and had done so since before the war. When the Fascist Party was formed in Milan in March 1919, Marinetti was elected to its Central Committee and in November was an unsuccessful candidate in parliamentary elections. Mussolini, who as early as 1914 had met Boccioni and expressed his great admiration for Futurism, sought the involvement of high-profile cultural figures such as Marinetti, the conductor Arturo Toscanini, and the poet and inspirer of Marinetti, Gabriele D'Annunzio who, famously, occupied the border town of Fiume for a year in 1919. Mussolini soon realised, however, that his big-name connections were not always helpful in attracting support and quickly began to distance himself from them. He could not afford to seem too involved with men such as Marinetti who, by 1920, was talking of a kind of anti-bourgeois and anti-papal revolution far too visionary and libertarian for Mussolini's pragmatic and authoritarian instincts.

Marinetti was equally suspicious of Mussolini whom he had described as early as January 1919 as 'a megalomaniac who will little by little become a reactionary'. Sadly for Marinetti, he needed Mussolini more than 'Il Duce' needed him. Marinetti and the Futurists contributed a great deal to Mussolini's efforts, through violence, agitation or propaganda, but they were to be disappointed by their eventual status within the Fascist state, which was indeed compromised and reactionary in a way utterly inimical to the Futurist ideal of 'elastic liberty'. When Marinetti resigned his position on the Central Committee in May 1920 after a theatrical exit from the second National Fascist Congress in Milan, his action ushered in a brief period of alignment with leftist politics, a return to the more artistic aspects of Futurism and an attempt to promote an 'Italian Revolution', more concerned with cultural freedom than its Russian counterpart. His hopes of working with Mussolini at the heart of the Fascist revolution were dashed, however, and from the middle of the 1920s, following Il Duce's proclamation of a Fascist dictatorship, Marinetti kept Futurism alive as a noisy and often brilliant and influential side-show to the new regime's cult of the great leader presented through an elaborate bureaucracy and a spectacle of modernised classicism and nostalgia for the order and imperial splendour of the Roman Empire. Even Marinetti was unable to avoid institutionalisation, becoming a member of the new 'Reale Accademia d'Italia' in 1929, joining other co-opted figures such as the musician Ottorino Respighi, the dramatist Luigi Pirandello and the inventor Guglielmo Marconi.

Mussolini's cultural policy with regard to the visual arts, however, was surprisingly open and allowed for a variety of tendencies, including Futurism. The neo-classicism and espousal of *Valori Plastici* (plastic values) of the 'Novecento' movement favoured by Mussolini's influential Jewish mistress,

Margherita Sarfatti, was pre-eminent during much of the Fascist era in Italy and represented a far more 'modern' kind of pictorial traditionalism than that which was vigorously promoted for ideological purposes in Nazi Germany in the 1930s. Former Futurists such as Carrà, Mario Sironi and Achille Funi were typical of those avant-gardists sympathetic to Fascism who reinvented the notion of 'Italianità' through a continuing engagement with modernism. Mussolini's cultural eclecticism, particularly in painting, sculpture, design and architecture was the result of his attempt to hold a volatile national culture in check, as well as a testimony to his instinct that Fascism should maintain at least a strong sense of imaginative adventure and that it should be identified in the popular consciousness with an optimistic 'modern style'. In this fairly liberal climate there was certainly room for Marinetti to manoeuvre. The

Futurist Congress organised by Mino Somenzi in Milan in 1924, while plagued by factional unrest and even violence, was a public display through discussion and grand processions of the Futurists' willingness to enter into a dialogue with Fascism. It is interesting to speculate, however, to what extent Marinetti and his followers may have looked back with nostalgia on the days of Giolitti's government. While Fascism was seen by many as the final and triumphant phase of the 'Risorgimento', and the end of liberal corruption in Italy, some Futurists may have wondered just how far their new masters had produced the conditions for a fresh and more vigorous period in Italian art and culture. Certainly Marinetti's coming out in favour of the monarchy in 1924 and his confession of his Catholic faith would have seemed a bizarre sign of the times in which they were now living.

As has been noted, the First World War and its aftermath left Marinetti with a depleted core of Futurist visual artists. Balla became, by default, the leading

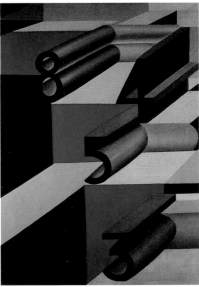

57
Mussolini (holding book) with Marinetti (centre), Traianei market, Rome 1932

58
Giacomo Balla
Numbers in Love 1920
Oil on panel
77 × 56
(30¼ × 22)
Private Collection

figure and, based in Rome, built on the relationship he had developed since 1915 with the artists Fortunato Depero and Enrico Prampolini. The art of the 'Second Futurism' produced by Balla and Depero in the 1920s is characterised by a decorative abstraction that employs volumetric forms and was particularly suited to architectural design, fashion, typography and scenography (fig.58). Continuing the aims expressed in their 'Futurist Reconstruction of the Universe' manifesto of 1915, Balla and Depero attempted to create a popular style that could be applied to all areas of life and could form the basis of a 'total' Futurist environment.

In 1929 Balla, Depero and Prampolini, along with Marinetti and his wife Benedetta, were among the signatories of a 'Manifesto of Aeropainting'. While Balla abandoned his Futurist allegiances shortly after this, Prampolini became the leading exponent of *aeropittura*. Living mainly in Paris between 1925 and 1937, Prampolini had wide contacts with avant-garde movements across Europe, from the Purist and Abstraction-Création artists in France to De Stijl in Holland and Constructivism in Russia. *Aeropittura*, as Prampolini practised it, was a semi-abstract form of painting that sought to convey the 'cosmic' poetry of flight, and to visualise through biomorphic shapes and evocative colour the transcendence of the spirit towards higher states of consciousness (fig.59). These spiritual aspirations even made it possible for Prampolini and others to contribute to exhibitions of *arte sacra* (sacred art) organised by the new Fascist cultural syndicates and the Catholic church. In spite of clerical hostility to such work, Marinetti and the painter known as Fillia (a pseudonym for Luigi Colombo, 1904–1936) were able to claim in 1931 that 'only Futurist aeropainters can make their canvases vibrate with impressions of the multi form and speedy life of angels in heaven and the apparition of saints'. While this may seem as surreal as some of Marinetti's recipes in his *Futurist Cookbook* of the following year ('Words-in-Freedom Sea Platter' and 'Simultaneous Ice-Cream' being two typical examples), it is also a salutary reminder that times change, ideas move in mysterious ways and even the most uncompromising radicals have to survive somehow.

Aeropittura picked up on a widespread contemporary fascination with aviators and all things aeronautical that can be seen in the films, novels and magazines of the period devoted to *aerovita*. As early as 1918 the Futurist Felice

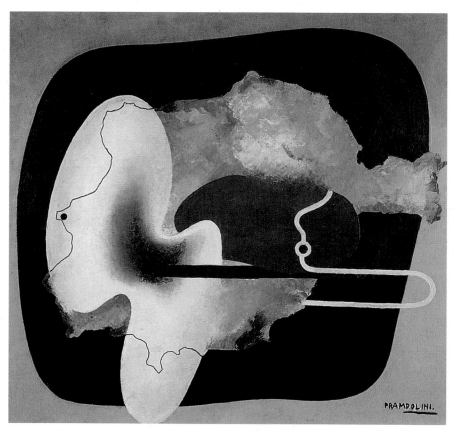

59
Enrico Prampolini

Extraterrestrial Spirituality 1932

Oil on board
48 × 52 (19 × 20½)
Private Collection

60
Tullio Crali

Dogfight I 1936–8
Oil on board
100 × 110 (39½ × 43¼)
Private Collection

Azari had 'choreographed' aerial dances in a plane, supported by Russolo's music, in the skies over Milan. Most European countries had their pilot-heroes and Italo Balbo in Italy, who crossed the Atlantic in 1931, was the nation's leading aviator and symbol of the Fascist future. Many *aeropittori* such as Tato (1896–1974) and Alfredo Ambrosi (1901–1945) exploited this popular enthusiasm with images that were far more literal and militaristic than those of avant-gardists such as Prampolini and Fillia. One of the most successful exhibitors at the many *aeropittura* exhibitions across Italy during the 1930s was Tullio Crali (b.1910) who, in works such as *Dogfight I* (fig.60), created images glorifying the Italian airforce in a form of popular illustration that nevertheless drew on elements of modernism to achieve its almost cinematic effects.

Marinetti fought long and hard to make Futurism an influential force across the whole spectrum of Italian culture between the wars. In many respects he was successful, particularly in the applied arts, even though the talent available to him was less impressive than that of his original cohorts. Regional movements from Turin to Sicily, not always loyal to Mussolini, kept the movement alive through exhibitions, events and publications and the Futurists led an admirable rearguard action against attempts by Fascist hardliners to introduce racist measures, based on Nazi policies, against 'degenerate art'. All this was achieved against a background of secret police surveillance of Marinetti and his colleagues and, as the political climate grew bleaker in the late 1930s, strenuous attempts to discredit the movement by its powerful enemies in the Ministry of Popular Culture. Marinetti himself, of course, was a committed Fascist, a patriot and a man of action; when Mussolini invaded Ethiopia in 1936 he did not hesitate to enlist as a volunteer at the age of sixty in the same spirit with which he had joined the army in 1915.

There was no avoiding the unpleasant truth for Marinetti, however, that by the end of the 1930s, despite the prevalence of Futurist cookery, fashion, ceramics, exhibition design and so on, Futurism had run out of steam. When war came in 1940, Marinetti became an unashamed apologist for the regime and Futurism degenerated into vulgar and inflammatory propaganda for the war effort, which often lapsed into the anti-semitism the movement had struggled against only a few years before. In 1940 Marinetti wrote of Mussolini thus: 'The duce radiant

ouside his body solid elastic ready to strike … continuously … accelerating towards the light … proud cosmic divinity of heroism and of invisible volcanoes but more than present applauded by his kinsmen with our throbbing hearts … stupendous choice of revolutionary prototypes.' Whatever Mussolini may have made of these sentiments, they led Marinetti to follow his hero to the bitter end, firstly by fighting on the Russian front in 1942 (fig.61), and then, in 1943, by joining the Republic of Salò, set up by the Germans following Italy's military defeat that year. When he died alone in his bed in Bellagio on 2 December 1944, a few months before Mussolini's execution, Marinetti was unrepentant in his commitment to Fascism. Like many artists and intellectuals, including Ezra Pound, who had moved to Italy in the 1920s and become a fanatical admirer of Mussolini, Marinetti believed, in the face of overwhelming evidence to the contrary, that an authoritarian regime offered the best chance of realising his radical aesthetic and ethical vision.

BIBLIOGRAPHY

SOURCES OF QUOTATIONS

Apollonio, Umbro, ed., *Futurist Manifestos*, London and New York 1973:
    BALLA: 'Futurist Manifesto of Men's Clothing' 1913, p.132
    BOCCIONI ET AL: 'Manifesto of the Futurist Painters' 1910, p.25; 'Futurist Painting: Technical Manifesto' 1910, pp.27–31; 'The Exhibitiors to the Public' (*Exhibition of Works by the Italian Futurist Painters*, exh. cat. Sackville Gallery, London 1912), p.46
    CARRÀ: 'The Painting of Sounds, Noises and Smells' 1913, p.114
    MARINETTI: 'Founding Manifesto of Futurism' 1909, pp.20–1, 23; 'Destruction of Syntax–Imagination Without Strings–Words-in-Freedom' 1913, pp.95–106; 'The Futurist Cinema' 1916, pp.207–19
    RUSSOLO: 'The Art of Noises' 1913, p.85
    DE SAINT-POINT: 'Futurist Manifesto of Lust' 1913, p.71
    SANT'ELIA: 'Manifesto of Futurist Architecture' 1914, pp.160–72.

Berghaus, Günter, *Futurism and Politics: Between Anarchist Rebellion and Fascist Reaction 1909–1944*, Providence and Oxford 1996:
    AMENDOLA: 'Il convegno nazionalista', *La Voce*, vol.2, no.51, Dec. 1910, p.6
    BOCCIONI ET AL: press release for Free Art Exhibition, Milan 1911, p.66
    CARLI *Noi Arditi*, 1919, p.103
    Document sent by Prefect of Milan 1914, p.75
    MARINETTI: 'Poema dei Sansepolcristi' 1940, p.261
    MARINETTI AND FILLIA: 'Manifesto of Futurist Sacred Art' 1931, p.245

Coen, Ester, *Umberto Boccioni*, exh. cat., Metropolitan Museum of Modern Art, New York 1988:
    letter to Barbarantini, autumn 1910, pp.94–6, 121
    letter to Severini, Nov. 1912, p.203

Flint, R.W., *Marinetti: Selected Writings*, London 1972:
    'Let's Murder the Moonlight', 1909, p.51
    'Against Passéist Venice' 1910, p.55
    'Futurist Speech to the English', 1910, pp.59–65
    'Techinical Manifesto of Futurist Literature' 1912, pp.84–5, 87, 89

Gray, Camilla, *The Russian Experiment in Art 1863–1922*, London 1986
    LARIONOV: 'Rayonnist Manifesto' 1913, pp.136–41

Hartt, Frederick, *Florentine Art under Fire*, Princeton 1949, p.47

Kern, Stephen, *The Culture of Time and Space 1880–1918*, Cambridge, Mass, 1983, p.1

Markov, Vladimir, *Russian Futurism: A History*, London 1969:
    KHLEBNIKOV/LIVSHITS: leaflet, p.151.

Nicholls, Peter, 'Futurism, Gender and Theories of Postmodernity', *Textual Practice*, vol.3, no.2, 1989, p.203

Tisdall, Caroline and Bozzolla, Angelo, *Futurism*, London 1977:
    BOCCIONI: war diary, 19 Oct.1915, p.180
    MARINETTI: *Zang Tumb Tumb* 1914, p.98
    SEVERINI: *Autobiography*, p.191

FURTHER READING

In addition to the works cited above, for those wishing to pursue an interest in Futurism the following books provide some pointers into the vast range of material now available. Many of them carry extensive bibliographies.

Antliff, Mark, *Inventing Bergson: Cultural Politics and the Parisian Avant-Garde*, Princeton 1993

Art and Power: Europe under the Dictators 1930–45 (compiled by Dawn Ades, Tim Benton, David Elliott, Iain Boyd Whyte), exh. cat., Hayward Gallery, London 1995

Banham, Peter Rayner, *Theory and Design in the First Machine Age*, London and New York 1960

Berghaus, Günther, *Italian Futurist Theatre 1909–1944*, Oxford 1998

Blum, Cinzia Sartini, *The Other Modernism: F.T. Marinetti's Futurist Fiction of Power*, California 1996

Corbett, David Peters, *The Modernity of English Art*, Manchester 1997

Cork, Richard, *Vorticism and Abstract Art in the First Machine Age*, 2 vols., London 1976

Futurism in Flight: 'Aeropittura' Paintings and Sculptures of Man's Conquest of Space 1913–1945, (eds. Bruno Mantura, Patrizia Rosazza-Ferraris and Livia Velani), exh. cat, Accademia Italiana, London 1990

Futurismo and Futurismi (ed. Pontus Hulten), exh. cat., Palazzo Grassi, Venice 1986

Hewitt, Andrew, *Fascist Modernism: Aesthetics, Politics, and the Avant-Garde*, Stanford 1993

Italian Art in the 20th Century: Painting and Sculpture 1900–1988 (ed. Emily Braun), exh. cat., Royal Academy of Arts, London 1989

Kirby, Michael, *Futurist Performance*, New York 1971

Marinetti, F.T., *The Futurist Cookbook*, London 1989

Martin, Marianne, *Futurist Art and Theory 1909–15*, Oxford 1968

Perloff, Marjorie, *The Futurist Moment: Avant-Garde, Avant-Guerre and the Language of Rupture*, Chicago and London 1986

Pound's Artists: Ezra Pound and the Visual Arts in London, Paris and Italy, with essays by Richard Humphreys, John Alexander and Peter Robinson, London 1985

Sternhell, Zeev (with Mario Sznajder and Maia Asheri), *The Birth of Fascist Ideology: From Cultural Rebellion to Political Revolution* (trans. David Maisel), Princeton 1994

Taylor, Christina, *Futurism: Politics, Painting and Performance*, Ann Arbor 1979

White, John J., *Literary Futurism: Aspects of the First Avant-Garde*, Oxford 1990

Wohl, Robert, *A Passion for Wings: Aviation and the Western Imagination 1908–1918*, New Haven and London 1994

PHOTOGRAPHIC CREDITS

ACRPP, Paris 1;
Bibliothèque Nationale de
France, Paris 9; from: Anton
Giulio Bragaglia, *Fotodinamismo
Futurista* © A. Vigliani
Bragaglia 25, 35; Bridgeman
Art Library, London 10, 13,
24, 37, 60; British Library,
London 48; Luca Carrà 54;
Civica Gallerie d'Arte
Moderna, Milan 6, 55;
Courtesy Anthony d'Offay
Gallery, London / photo:
Prudence Cuming Associates
Ltd 45; Foto Saporetti,
Milan 8; Galleria Nazionale
d'Arte Moderna, Rome /
photo: Giuseppe Schiavinotto
56; Haags Gemeentemuseum,
The Hague 22; The Kobal
Collection / photo: Jonathan
Wenk 4; Musei Civici di
Como 2; © Museum of
Modern Art, New York 11,
14, 17–21; Musei Civici di
Torino 27; Scala 12; © The
Solomon R. Guggenheim
Foundation 53; Stedelijk
Museum, Amsterdam 50, 52;
Tate Gallery Photographic
Department, London 7, 15,
28–9, 31–3, 39–43, 46–7, 49, 51;
Victoria and Albert Museum,
London 26

COPYRIGHT CREDITS

INDEX